POLARIS ADVISORY GROUP, LLC

COMMON SENSE BUSINESS
A COMPENDIUM OF WHITE PAPERS
WITH PRACTICAL ADVICE   FOR
MANAGING YOUR BUSINESS

George E. Devitt

TABLE OF CONTENTS

FOREWORD

For seven years, Polaris Advisory Group has been sending e-Mail messages to the leaders of organizations around the country. Every two weeks or so, about 70,000 of these messages go out with a subject which we hope is both topical and relevant. For each of these messages, we develop a White Paper which provides more in-depth information than is contained in the message itself.

To receive the White Paper(s), which are offered at no charge, the recipient of the message simply clicks on a "HyperLink" which takes him or her to a short e-form on our web-site which asks for some very basic information – name, e-Mail address, role, etc.

Many of those who receive our semi-monthly e-Mail messages consistently click on the link and request our White Papers. But an analysis of our web-site statistics shows that far more people read our messages than "click through" to our web-site. And frankly, this is understandable. We all get e-Mail messages with "links" that may take us to somewhere on the vast World Wide Web which will result in our computer becoming infected with a virus.

We also know that many people feel that by completing the form they will receive persistent and pesky follow-up calls in which someone on our team may try to sell something. We've never done that at Polaris, and never will. But the reader of the e-Mail doesn't know that.

For these and other reasons, we have assembled a "Compendium" of some eighty or so of our most requested White Papers. Some are simple one-page tips on, for example, "15 Things You Can Do to Ensure You Give a Killer Presentation." Others may be several pages long and make the case for implementing a "Major Account Program" or developing a documented Business Plan. Some may appeal more to the CFO and others to the Chief Marketing Officer.

But our belief is that all of them appeal and are relevant for the senior-most leader of the organization. And our research bears this out. From time-to-time, we will hire a third-party to contact the leader and ask directly. The evidence is clear that many of the Chairmen, Presidents and CEOs who receive our messages find them to be relevant, informative and topical.

Frankly, many of the things we cover are common sense. But most of us need an occasional "nudge" or a reminder. For example, almost every sales professional learned early in his or her career to send a follow-up letter after meeting with a customer executive – especially if it's the first meeting. But over time, we know that what was once a habit is now rarely completed.

Common sense permeates almost all of our White Papers (and by calling our documents by this name we are most assuredly doing a disservice to the academic treatises which are more accurately so named). But readers tell us that they generally get one or two good "nuggets" from each. And because most of our documents are rooted in common-sense and have practical applications, we've decided to entitle this book Common Sense Business. We're pretty confident that you'll get several of your own "nuggets" from reading it. And that alone will make our publishing it worthwhile.

POLARIS
ADVISORY GROUP

3 Cost-Efficient Steps Leading to an
Effective Competitive Intelligence Program

Some big companies have entire departments devoted to gathering competitive intelligence. Yet even companies which haven't reached that threshold yet can get a leg up on the competition through online research -- and the cooperation of key people.

The key, experts say, is that you don't get so wrapped up in gathering information that you wait too long to act. Early on in your research into a competitor's upcoming product launch, you may have the opportunity to develop a new product yourself or close out your competitor's distribution channel. But the longer you wait, the fewer options you'll have to respond to a competitor's move.

Experts also caution entrepreneurs not to lie or misrepresent themselves or who they work for. Read up on the Economic Espionage Act, because it governs the legalities of gathering competitive intelligence. If your company has an ethics policy, make sure you understand it and adhere to it. If it doesn't have a formal ethics policy, caution is the watchword.

The three steps:

1. Mine the free research online.

Databases
Start with Google.com. But be sure to use other search engines to find the one that gives the best results for your industry.

On Google and AltaVista, type in "link: www.whatevercompanyyouwant.com" and you will get a list of Web Sites that link to the specified company's Web site. It's a good way to find out the companies that have an interest in or are doing business with the company you're researching.

InvisibleWeb.com is a directory of more than 10,000 databases, archives, and search engines. Use it to research companies, industries, and business publications.

Northern Light conducts searches of industry-focused Web pages, market research, economic analysis, and company reports. It also sells research by the page, so you can buy only the pages you need, instead of having to buy the entire report. Before you pay for information, check whether you can get the same information for free from another site, such as PR Newswire.

Marketresearch.com is a collection of more than 40,000 publications from more than 350 leading research firms.

2. Enlist the help of everyone at your company and as many customers, vendors, and others as possible.

You can do a lot of research on the Internet, but talking to people remains the best way to gather intelligence. Ask your employees to be your eyes and ears in the marketplace, in your industry -- even in your company's reception area.

Your receptionist can be one of your most valuable resources. In one of our clients in which the purchasing manager routinely keeps vendors waiting for 10 to 15 minutes after they arrive, the receptionist writes down what the vendors talk about. Sometimes they talk about the deal they'll offer to the company. The receptionist e-mails that information to the purchasing manager, so he is better prepared for the negotiations.

Capitalizing on internal resources is the single best way to conduct competitive intelligence. Leverage the relationships your employees have with other folks in your industry, especially their colleagues from previous jobs. Consider approaching company employees who are knowledgeable, but undervalued as resources of competitive information, such as an accountant or quality assurance manager.

To help employees know what kind of information you're after, circulate a list of the factors that are critical to your company's success. Ask them to keep their eyes and ears open and report back relevant information.

Another client eschews online research and focuses on letting every employee and customer know that he values tips they pass on to him. "The more people who know you care and what you care about, the more information you're going to get," this CEO says. He once kept a distributor from taking business away from him by confronting the distributor after a customer told him that the distributor had offered him a better deal. At a trade show, this CEO discovered that the distributor was doing everything he could to gain business, even at a low margins. He told the distributor directly that "it isn't fair to steal someone else's customers." The distributor backed off – knowing the value of channel partnerships and not violating the ethics associated with a multi-tier distribution model.

3. Cultivate relationships with key experts.

Identify experts in your industry or market and develop a relationship with them. The Web can help you identify experts, but it's no substitute for a personal relationship.

Gaining access to experts helps you keep ahead of published reports. Be sure that you send these experts interesting information that you come across, so you are offering help as well as asking for it.

In order to get information, you may have to give information. You need to know where to draw the line on giving out information. You're going to be much more interesting to talk to if you have a bone you can throw them. It's good to practice role-plays with your colleagues and prepare comebacks, but don't be surprised if you're rebuffed.

The most promising sources to cultivate are:

- **Securities analysts**. They are especially helpful for researching public companies. However, they may follow private companies if the companies are big players in their industries.

Use *Nelson's Directory of Investment Research*, available at business libraries, to find names of analysts.

- **Associations**. They can be very valuable, especially if you want to learn about an industry. Association membership lists can help you identify suppliers. Some associations will send you their membership directory, even if you're not a member. Find names of associations in the *Encyclopedia of Associations*, usually available at public libraries. (Consult the **American Society of Association Executives** for information on associations in a variety of industries.)

- **Journalists**. This is especially true of local, small-town journalists. Look for places where a target company is a big fish in a small pond. If a Fortune 500 company has a plant in a small town, people in that town will be very interested in what's going on at the company and may be willing to talk to you. Then you can use that information as fodder for conversations with people at the corporate office. Because only a small percentage of any interview makes it into print, journalists know a lot more than what's in their articles.

  Go to **Bizjournals.com** to find local business journals. To find other print publications, consult *The Standard Periodical Directory*, available at public libraries. Call the local paper and ask the business editor who covers the company you're interested in. If there are photos with a story, talk to the photographer, especially if photos were taken inside a manufacturing facility.

Bigger isn't necessarily better when it comes to doing competitive research. Big companies might have entire departments dedicated to the endeavor, but smaller companies have the speed, drive, and dedication to get it done.

POLARIS
ADVISORY GROUP

3 Habits Of Highly Effective Leaders

Are you in a leadership position? Whether you're an executive or an entry-level employee, leadership is a truly essential skill that can propel you and your career to bigger, better things. That holds true for both leaders of large teams and self-employed people who are guiding a team of one.

Three habits a competent leader practices regularly.

The first habit is asking different questions. This is about expanding your curiosity. The second habit is taking multiple perspectives. This habit is about listening well and understanding the perspectives of others. The third habit is looking at systems, and that one reminds us that while the human brain likes to break things down into manageable parts, it is the unwieldy combination of those unmanageable systems that opens us up to new possibilities.

Do even the best leaders make mistakes?

Of course! They'll get mad and make mistakes and hurt people. And sometimes they won't even recognize that they've done that. But the best leaders never stop learning. They never become so arrogant or complacent that they stop believing they have room to grow. They never become so hopeless or discouraged that they believe it's not worth the effort. John F. Kennedy wrote that "leadership and learning are indispensable to each other." The good leaders never forget this.

What else separates great leaders from everyone else?

They create environments where people can be at their "biggest." We all have the experience of people who make us smaller and less capable versus those who make us more capable in their presence than we are without them. Good leaders remember that their perspective isn't the only truth, and they welcome entire human beings into the workplace -- inconvenient emotions, vague hunches, thoughtless mistakes and all. When people see us in our messy wholeness, we can spread out and become bigger.

If I want to become more of a leader today, how should I start?

The most important thing is to <u>believe</u> that you can change and begin to look for the ways you might need to by asking for feedback from others. Forgive yourself for your limitations (rather than denying them or beating yourself up about them), and then seek to grow beyond the way you understand the world today. Great leaders seek 360-degree feedback on how they're doing – and they adapt and change as a result of that feedback.

POLARIS
ADVISORY GROUP

3 Keys to Turning Your Pipeline into Revenue

At first blush, the logic is sound. The more calls you make, the more prospects will become interested in your product or service. The more interested prospects you have, the more sales you'll make. The more sales you make, the more revenue you'll generate. Thus, more calls will yield more revenue. Put another way, "…the more 'no's' you get, the closer you'll be to getting a 'yes.'"

While this may be true, it's not the most effective way to approach an individual's sales territory or an organization's market. Our approach focuses more on the *quality* of the sales pipeline than the *quantity* of prospects in the pipeline, developing a strategy for making yourself *relevant* to the prospective buyer and *executing* your strategy with discipline.

Build a Quality Pipeline

Take the time to research your prospect's business online prior to reaching making a call. Leverage social media information that you can find on LinkedIn, Facebook and Twitter. While it is tempting to create as large a pipeline as possible in the hope that high numbers will produce high sales, this is not the most effective or efficient way to approach your territory or your firm's markets. If your company, product or service isn't relevant to the prospective customer, calling will only dilute your focus on the best opportunities.

Think about whether or not your prospect looks like your ideal customer and build your pipeline with prospects that you know are a fit for your products or services. Be honest about deleting and adding to it every day. This targeted group is the pool from which you will generate actual sales and revenues.

Sales Strategy: Make Yourself Relevant

The Internet provides you the opportunity to research your prospect's business goals, objectives, competitive environment, and leadership. Based on this, you can align your own organization with the prospective customer's business in your initial contact. In today's environment in which people are being asked to do more with less, they're busier than ever. Making your initial contact compelling and relevant is crucial to breaking through the "clutter" of calls and e-mails that every customer gets.

LinkedIn is a valuable social media tool to determine the right people to contact within your prospective customer organization, as well as something about their background and work history. If you can find the same people on other social media sites, such as Facebook, you can learn some personal information about the individual contact, such as his or her interests, activities and hobbies. Using this information provides you the opportunity to connect on a personal – as well as professional – level.

Disciplined Execution of Your Strategy

It's imperative that the sales professional develop a well-planned, consistent and proactive outbound plan to ensure success.

Because you've developed a targeted list of prospective customers, you know that these prospects are a network of professionals to whom you can offer help. Reach out to them with a phone call, a LinkedIn message or an e-mail. If you don't contact them directly, leave a VoiceMail followed up by an e-mail introducing yourself and your company and explain to them why you believe they should take a few minutes to speak with you. You might try a message like this:

- "Hi Mr./Ms. Prospect, my name is Jo Seller, calling from Acme Sales. We specialize in providing drilling solutions to companies like yours. In fact, for one company similar to yours, we were able to provide a solution which resulted in reduced drilling costs of 13% and increased yields of 18%. After researching your company, I have some ideas that may help your firm achieve similar results. I'd welcome the opportunity to share some of these ideas, as well as what we've been seeing in the market, to determine if we might be able to offer something of value to your firm. Do you have 10 minutes to connect over the phone this week or next?"

Give them a compelling reason to speak with you, not a "pie-in-the-sky" marketing pitch. These people get calls every day, and if you don't sound like someone who can add value, they will not take the time to speak with you. You have to stand out – and making yourself relevant is the key to doing this.

Always fine-tune your message for each industry segment and job function. Don't use one boiler-plate message for every call. Customize, personalize, individualize, and optimize your calls. Engage interested prospects, and move those who are not ready to buy into a "nurturing" mode. Always keep in mind that it is your job to add value on every call.

Set a goal for each day. And don't base it on the number of "dials" made each day. Base your goal on the number of meaningful conversations you complete each day that result in qualified prospects.

Summary

It's our experience that those sales professionals and sales organizations which develop a pipeline of high-quality prospects, who make themselves relevant to those prospects, and who practice the discipline of setting and achieving daily, weekly and monthly goals are winners every time.

Three Reasons Many Executives
<u>Think Sales Training Doesn't Work</u>

For a topic like this one, the first item to accept and acknowledge is that the fundamental truth of the premise needs to be addressed. Given that in the United States millions of dollars are spent each year on sales training, are there significant numbers of influential people who think that sales training really doesn't work.

Answer: yes.

But yes needs a bit of explanation. First, there are companies who do sales training, think it's an okay thing to do, but don't really think it is going to make a big impact on their bottom lines. Indicators of this point of view are statements such as: "We haven't done any training for a while, it's about time." or "I'm sure our people will at least learn one thing from the sales training." or "We have that time slot at are national meeting, we should consider doing some sales training."

Other companies seldom or never do any sales training. Given the dynamics of today's markets with customers going through transformational changes, more new products being introduced every day, and companies launching major shifts in their go-to-market strategies, it is hard to believe that lack of a need is the reason for not doing or postponing sales training.

So why do people think sales training doesn't work? Although there are a number of infrequently occurring whys and wherefores, three reasons can explain most of the rationale behind the "it doesn't work" point of view.

Let's examine each of the reasons and in closing explore why it might be worth taking a second look – that is, maybe it does work.

- **Bad Experiences.** If you talk with those who make the sales training decision, Directors of Training and VPs of Sales, a modest number have had one or more past bad experiences implementing a sales training effort.

Some of these bad experiences have been just sort of bad – "Our people like the sales training and said it was useful but six months later nobody was doing anything different." On the other hand, some experiences were really bad – "The content was the same old stuff – the examples and cases were all generic –and the design was just a pile of PowerPoints – our people went nuts."

Once bitten, twice shy. Unfortunately this idiom is ever so true when it comes to doing something where you put your money and reputation on the line.

But explore the story behind the story and the reasons for these failures have several explanations. For example, in some cases the actual training was okay but the implementation and/or reinforcement was poorly done.

Unfortunately in a significant number of cases the negative attitude is the result of **sales training's checkered past.** If you look to the past, a number of sales training programs were based on magic and myths. As an alert, some of these programs have escaped into the future.

- **Lack of Proof.** Some people make the decision about whether something works based on whether there is any solid research that proves that it works.

When the search for that evidence is carried out in regard to sales training, the results tend to be meager at best. Has some solid work been done? Yes, for example, researcher Neil Rackham did some great research in behavioral analysis when he created the SPIN model and more recently, the folks who did the work around the Challenger Sale backed it up with some credible research.

But in the main there is not a lot of solid stuff out there. Individual companies sometimes do the substantial research and evaluation work but it is usually not accessible. Alternatively, the work that is available is frequently just opinion surveys or self-promotional studies.

So as they say – fair enough. But there is another side to the story. First, it is good to remember that sales training is a social, not physical, science. Therefore the pre-post control group type research designs are not really applicable. Second, if one went looking for that same level of research in regard to compensation frameworks, CRM systems, or needs assessments the same lack of results would likely be the outcome – that is sales training has some good company.

If you are looking for hard research data as proof of the payback on sales training, you're not going to find it. The next best approach is to do a really good job talking with other folks who have used that program for which you are about to write a check. This means going beyond the one phone call. Talk with multiple companies and multiple people inside those companies. In addition make sure you see an example of the training materials or see a program.

- **Unique Need.** This reason is a little bit different. It usually comes from people who think that sales training can work. They have often already done sales training that was effective in the fundamentals like sales call execution skills, account strategy, or sales negotiation. But now they are facing performance issues that are more unique and complex and they doubt whether sales training can help.

If one has not recently reviewed what is available in the sales training world, then this conclusion is substantially correct. In the past a significant number of the sales training programs were generic or at best semi-customized. Regardless of the problem, the sales training solution was fundamentally the same. And, the different programs were really not that different.

Clearly as we can see there are some legitimate reasons for people holding the point of view that sales training doesn't work.

The good news is a tremendous amount of work has been accomplished in the last several years to design a new era of sales training programs. Today's sales training is not your father's Oldsmobile. Plus, there are now more training vendors with which to partner to custom-design programs that are tailored to your unique needs in a cost-effective fashion.

Our best suggestion – take a second look. Best bet – if you think it doesn't work you may be pleasantly surprised.

POLARIS
ADVISORY GROUP

3 Simple Tips to a Killer Presentation!

#1. Get a hook! Most audiences rush to conclusions in the first two minutes of your presentation. Failure to develop a solid introduction is one of the biggest mistakes sales professionals make. Leverage those first two minutes to take command of your listeners. Engage them with a relevant story. Grab their attention with an alarming insight. Or just make them smile with some simple humor. Worry less about educating (do you like to be educated?) and worry more about entertaining (everyone likes to be entertained). I'm not suggesting you start your next presentation with a card trick (although that could be a great hook). But I am suggesting you take a hard look at how you get your audience to lean in for the first two minutes of your next presentation. Script, practice and polish your hook until it is rock solid. Grabbing their attention from the very start sets you and your ideas apart from everyone else who just "wings" their opening. And a great hook creates confidence that you can build upon throughout your presentation.

#2. "I know this next slide is a little hard to read"
PowerPoint was originally developed to be a visual aid; a tool that presenters could use to add "power" to their message by highlighting a key "point." Think big fonts, few words, maybe even a picture or two to drive home important ideas. PowerPoint was not designed to be a proposal tool or a script. Save the Gantt charts for the appendix... PLEASE! PowerPoint decks aren't the presentation, you are the presentation. The deck is there to support you and your ideas. Look at it another way. PowerPoint decks that are jammed full of data, charts, conclusions and complete paragraphs could just be emailed to the customer. What do they need you for? The customer can read it themselves and it saves you from having to make a sales call. What an interesting way to decrease business and work yourself out of a job.

#3. The two words that everyone loves to close with. Most of the sales presentations I get to watch (and I get to watch plenty) close with the presenter saying "thank you." Not exactly a strong call to action, is it? You deliver presentations because you want someone to do something. You might want their approval or an introduction or maybe you want their feedback on an idea. The bottom line is you want something from your listener and the best way to get it is to ask for it! I know you won't always get what you want, but if you'll ask for something specific it becomes a springboard for questions, discussion and next steps. You walk out of the board room knowing where you stand versus going back to the office and hoping that your phone will ring.

3 Steps to Converting Leads into Sales

To achieve maximum ROI on your lead-generation programs, we recommend this 3-step strategy:

1) **Make contact as soon as possible.** If you wait too long, leads might forget who you are – or worse, assume you don't think they're worth your time. We recommend "scoring" the prospects based on demographics, activity history and online behavioral triggers. This allows your sales team to follow up on the highest-potential leads first, while allowing marketing to nurture the rest.

2) **Keep in regular contact with leads.** Don't send an email, however, unless it has content they'll consider relevant. Send pertinent messages related to where your prospect is in the buying cycle. And offer information to help move them from one stage in the "sales funnel" to the next.

3) **Be sure your in-house teams talk to each other.** Your pipeline will stagnate if Marketing and Sales don't establish an ongoing dialogue about the parameters for qualification. Remember: those

parameters can be cyclical, and are likely to change as a sales department's priorities change.

The point is this: to turn leads into sales, be one of the <u>three in ten</u> companies actively nurturing their leads.

Increasing Forecasting Accuracy by Selling Value

Much has been written about "Value-Based-Selling." The methodology has many different names associated with it, but all of the variations are essentially the same. The premise is quite simple: by quantifying, in dollar terms, the benefits of your product, service or solution and comparing these benefits to the costs (or the "investment") required by your customer, a compelling "Business Case" can be made to support your sales efforts.

In fact, the stronger the Business Case, the greater the urgency which should be associated with the purchasing action by the customer. That urgency may result from foregone revenues or in foregone cost savings resulting from the customer delaying the purchase, depending upon the nature of the business case. But whether the product or service increases the customer's revenues or reduces its expenses, a solid business case will instill a sense of urgency, because in either case, prolonging the purchase results in lost profits.

The phrase, "It's not a matter of if, but when," for most of the world is a compelling and calming message. The idea that something IS going to happen is adequate enough. It makes most of us comfortable and alleviates the stress of the unknown. But in the sales profession, "when" something is going to happen, is as important as "if" something is going to happen. And if you can't nail the when, you're only doing half your job.

Knowing when a customer is going to buy is less about if they want to buy and more about why they want to buy. Customers want a lot of things; however, actually making the purchase is built on why they want the product or service and the impact the purchase will have on the "current state." In other words, the customer may want the product or service because it will increase revenues or because it will decrease costs. Delaying the purchase means the customer forgoes these increased revenues or decreased costs; that is, there is some "pain" associated with delaying the purchase. The degree of this pain – or the amount of the profits reduced by a delayed purchase – will determine the urgency with which the customer will act. The greater the pain, the sooner the customer is likely to purchase.

This pain alone determines the speed of change. The greater the pain, the quicker the sale is made. The less pain that exists, the slower the sales process will be.

It's shaky ground if all we know is that the prospect *likes* the solution, if they say they want it or if they think it's a perfect fit, if you don't know why they need to change in the first place. Without knowing why a customer is thinking about changing, you don't know how big their problem is, and more importantly, how quickly they need to change to alleviate the "pain."

Need and desire to change are directly correlated with the speed at which a company changes. The more important the "new state" is to attain or the more important it is to leave the "current state," the faster the customer or prospect is going to move.

Knowing when your customers and prospects are going to buy is rooted squarely in the level of pain they are experiencing and their motives for change. Spend your time trying to understand why your customer wants to change and what would happen if they didn't. If change isn't compelling, or if you can't clearly articulate the importance of the new state, understanding when they will make the decision becomes very difficult and makes forecasting with any degree of accuracy almost impossible.

So – why isn't Value-Based-Selling used as a matter of course in every sales situation? The answers lay in the nature of the product or service. For example, the manufacturer of the inkjet cartridges for my desktop printer doesn't have to "sell the value" of my purchasing replacement cartridges. If my cartridges are out of ink, I can't print – so no cost-justification is necessary. In these situations, the seller of the cartridges doesn't need to sell the value of the cartridge to justify the purchase, but faces a different value-related challenge: for example, why should I pay the higher price for a brand name cartridge when an off-label product is ostensibly just as good?

In general, however, the more "commodity-like" the product, the more the value discussion will be related to the benefits of the "brand." Frankly, these decisions are based more on emotions than on any quantifiable difference in value. A customer may "feel" more comfortable purchasing, for example, a printer cartridge manufactured by Hewlett-Packard than one which is in an Office Depot box. It is for this reason that vendors in the "commodity-like" space invest in building their brand, creating a consumer preference for their products and causing consumers to associate certain attributes with their brand which – for some – will justify a higher price. In this example, while the "Office Depot" product may in fact be manufactured by Hewlett-Packard on the <u>exact same assembly line</u> as the HP-branded product, consumers may associate the HP product as more reliable and dependable, and thus worth the higher price.

In situations in which the product is new, revolutionary, or represents "breakthrough innovation," consumers will likely associate a greater value with it, justifying a higher price. The iPhone is a good example of this, although this perception of greater value is generally limited to a period of time sufficient for competitors to respond with products offering similar functionality, so these companies must act with alacrity to derive the benefits of their breakthrough.

To summarize:

- Quantify the increased revenues or decreased costs associated with your product or service for the customer and communicate this in terms of a business case to the customer or prospective customer;
- Determine the urgency associated with your product or service from the perspective of the customer, i.e., assess the "pain" associated with not purchasing your product and "rank-order" the pain associated with your product or service against other, competing investment opportunities available to the customer;
- When there are competing products which are highly similar to those offered by your firm, determine those emotive values in which your firm has an advantage and assign a value associated with each. In fact, we've found it to be highly effective when we ask the customer to assign such a value. For example, if your product is demonstrably more reliable or your customer service and support are demonstrably superior – and assuming that the customer would concur – with the customer, make a list of these factors or considerations and then, in an interactive fashion, ask the customer to quantify the degree of your firm's superiority for each factor.

Imagine meeting with the customer and asking him or her what areas he or she thinks your product has an advantage. And then, for example, if the customer says that your turnaround time for replacement parts is better than a competing alternative, ask "how much better?" Ask, for example, what the cost is for an hour of down-time for a production line and how many hours of down-time occur in an average month. Then, multiply the average number of hours of down-time per month by the cost of each hour of down time. After calculating the resulting number, multiply that by the percentage the customer attributed to your firm's superiority. In doing so, you've taken a seemingly "soft-dollar" benefit to a quantifiable value which can be used in justifying a premium price.

In sales, knowing if the customer will purchase AND when, are what we're paid for. Just because your customer "wants" something doesn't mean they are ready to buy it. That decision comes from an entirely different place. Start spending as much time as you can understanding when they will buy, not just if they will buy. Your manager will thank you for it.

POLARIS
ADVISORY GROUP

4 Critical Elements of Every Actionable Win/Loss Analysis

Top sales professionals know their capture and loss ratio. Why do they know it? Because, they understand that without good win/loss/no decision data, they have limited information about their sales trends. 'A' Players want to know if wins are trending with lower profitability. They want to know if the sales cycle is lengthening or shortening. They wonder which market segments, verticals, and company sizes are providing them the most success. All of this leads to better usage of the sales professional's efforts, and more wins in the long run.

How This Applies to You

Winning more deals is the obvious key to success for an individual, as well as a company. How this is achieved is the part that is less obvious (and more indicative of success). So what's the plan?

Flip conventional wisdom: Use a win/loss analysis **to structure your next deal.** Differentiation is always crucial to winning more deals. Using a win/loss analysis as the basis of your entire sales structure could do just that. Stand out above the competition by knowing what will or will not work with your prospect.

Why You Need a Win/Loss Analysis

1. **Continuous Improvement.** The landscape is always changing, and you need to keep up with those changes. First, market conditions aren't improving. Secondly, the competition is continuing to grow in size and strength – don't expect that to stop. Third, customers realize they no longer need to pound a path to your door. You have to find ways to bring them to you, and then convert them before someone else does.

2. **Problem Diagnosis.** World class companies perform win/loss analyses regularly. Why? They realize it is a very useful tool. It helps them discover weaknesses and eliminate them. Likewise, they can identify strengths and continue to capitalize on them. If you don't keep up with this practice, you'll end up out of the game. Don't be left behind because you didn't realize the importance of this tool in bettering yourself and your organization.

3. **Competitive Advantage.** In the event that your competitors aren't utilizing a Win/Loss Analysis you've got a major leg up. How, you ask? It will clearly separate you in the eyes of the buyer by providing you with insight into what specific prospects will be most receptive to. This will lead to more wins. This in turn separates you from the rest of the field.

What does a World Class Win/Loss Analysis Look Like?

It incorporates 4 distinct factors:

1. **360 Degree View** – A 360 Degree view compiles an assessment through the eyes of your customer that provides transparency into the reasons why sales opportunities are won, lost, or receive no decision.

   This is crucial for a number of reasons. Too many firms want to focus on the big loss and why it got away. This is certainly important. But you also need to know your wins, why they may be trending in a particular direction, or if you ideal customer profile is changing.

   A good 360 Degree View will focus on all outcomes:

   1. **Wins:** Great resource to watch trends and understand what is working in your market, segment, territory, etc.

   2. **Losses:** Losses can point to a weakness in your product, support service, maintenance, or sales process.

   3. **No Decision:** Uncover trends that might otherwise go un-noticed (but that doesn't make them any less important). Perhaps funding is drying up in your market? All of a sudden the key to selling is to provide financing or purchase terms.

2. **Timely** – Whenever possible the interviews should be done shortly after the buyer has made the decision. This is important for three reasons:
   a) Customers are most receptive to sharing this information at this time. The buyer may be basking in the comfort of knowing that the decision is made and feel less threatened about sharing the information.

b) The accuracy of the information will be highest when collected quickly.

c) By gathering data shortly after the event, you help to position yourself better for the next deal. You know how to adjust your offering if necessary. This works whether you won or lost the previous deal. Human psychology is an interesting thing. Rest assured that if you're quick to follow through with the customer, then you're putting yourself one step ahead of the competition.

3. **Tied to CRM –** It's easiest to maintain this win/loss data as part of your CRM archive. As customers progress through the buyer's journey, this can be set as the event trigger for your interviews. When an opportunity is converted to won, lost or closed, an interview can be initiated automatically so the information is captured in a timely manner.

4. **Independent –** Win/Loss best practice is to have the interview conducted by an independent 3rd party. If that's not possible, then solicit the help of your marketing department to manage this process. They are one step removed from sales and have a better chance of obtaining data from the buyer. Third parties can also be objective, which leads to better data and analysis.

As with many sales techniques and tools, just the act of undertaking an effort such as a win/loss analysis will put you a cut above the rest. Getting the right team to perform this analysis can spell the difference in making your numbers and not.

4 Elements of a Practical Approach to Pricing

Founders don't spend enough time examining pricing. They're too busy working on more important issues such as releasing version 2.0 and raising enough capital to keep the doors open. Brilliant entrepreneurs who build useful products generate substantial value, but in order to capture this value, they must implement rational pricing strategies. If you're one of these entrepreneurs, here's a quick guide on how to get started on pricing and avoid the most common traps:

1)   **Study your competitors**. There's no reason to reinvent the wheel. Even if you're stronger, faster or prettier, it's safe to say your competitors have done some homework already. Research competitive products' websites and go through their purchase processes. Ask some of your prospects or beta users how they evaluate products or services in your space and what their decision flow is like. Is the customer accustomed to modular or all-in-one pricing? Are there price tiers? How steep are volume discounts? Note surprises and nuances that apply to your business model.

2)   **Launch softly with a high "introductory" price**. The concept of an "introductory" prices powerful because it grants leeway for adjustment, yet also creates a sense of urgency that drives business through the door. Circulate this price freely among beta users, email subscribers and other ready-to-buy prospects.
Your introductory price should be enough to cover costs, but there's no need to stop there. Consider pricing your product at the high end of your comfort zone. Although it's hard to increase your prices once they're in circulation, you can readily reduce

them. Furthermore, a high introductory price sends a signal to the market that you have a quality product.

3)   **Over time, test a cross-section of lower price points**. Once you're comfortable that prospects understand your pricing model and your price point is in the right ballpark, you can periodically lower your prices through one-time discounts and product bundles. It becomes easier to fine-tune your pricing as volume increases.

One handy way to price test is to divide your prospect e-mail addresses into random buckets, issue coupons and measure total revenue generated. For example, test four coupons: $59.95, 69.95, 79.95 and 89.95. Customers reimbursed the highest proportion of $59.95 coupons, but the $69.95 coupons generated the most revenue, so this would indicate that prices should be lowered accordingly. If your firm is lacking a big prospect database, you might perform a similar test by striking through old prices on your purchase page, offering new prices each week for four consecutive weeks, measuring the revenue generated, and adjusting prices accordingly.

4)   **Finally, examine pricing attributes in the context of your overall business**.

- *Published pricing is a blessing and a curse.* In most B2B companies, price awareness lowers the friction for silent prospects who are close to purchasing, but it also diminishes your flexibility. If you choose to publish pricing, you can avoid boxing yourself in by requiring expensive price tiers and high-volume customers to contact you for information.

- *Free and "freemium" models drive growth at the expense of short-term profitability.* If you can afford it, consider giving away parts of your product or service for free. Explore capacity-based freemium models, which require customers to pay beyond a usage threshold, as well as feature-based freemium models, which provide free basic features, yet charge for premium features.

- A little grace goes a long way. You don't need to immediately penalize customers for exceeding price tiers or breaching license agreements. To your customer, there's nothing worse than logging in to find a big red X or coming back from vacation to realize service has been discontinued. Utilize grace periods and friendly messaging to keep customers happy so they become evangelists and refer more customers.

POLARIS

ADVISORY GROUP

4 Things Successful Executives Measure

1. Logging keeps you accountable. The first step is to determine the "what matters?" Some refer to these as KPI's (Key Performance Indicators). And these can (and probably should) include both personal and professional items. Quite simply, it answers the question, "At the end of the day, what are those things that I should accomplish and know that I've been successful?" If your logging doesn't reflect that you're spending sufficient time on those things that matter most, it's probably time to re-think how you spend your time.

2. Accountability boosts willpower. When you've identified the "what matters?" and aligned those against how you're spending your time, you will naturally have more willpower to devote the appropriate amount of time to those things that matter most.

3. Logging makes you mindful. When I had a look at the first log that I kept, I was shocked at how much time I spent on e-mail. I still haven't determined whether e-mail is a bane to my existence or a blessing. One thing I know, though, is that e-mail is inherently "reactive" in nature, and on my "what matters?" list is being more "pro-active." Time for an adjustment.

4. Metrics make you better. It's been said that "you can't manage what you can't measure." Metrics make you a better, more effective leader and manager. Simply by keeping track of the metrics that matter most to you and how they align with how you spend your time will make you better.

POLARIS
ADVISORY GROUP

4 Top Resources Used by Elite
Sales Professionals to Gain Their Edge

1 - A key trait of top quartile sales leaders is their ability to ask for help. They tap into external resources and get multiple perspectives. These often untapped third party resources that can give top sales professionals an extra "edge" come from unbiased resources from outside their own organization, and include:

1) Customers
2) Prospects
3) Outside firms that provide advice
4) Professional networks

How should these resources be utilized? For example, listen to your customers and prospects in a formalized manner. This is the best way to get real time feedback. Often sales professionals don't know the true reason they lose a deal. Nothing allows you to make improvements with more confidence than direct customer feedback. We believe that a Win/Loss Analysis is the best way to accomplish this and that at least five "wins" and five "losses" are evaluated every quarter. Third party firms such as Polaris Advisory Group can be helpful in this area due to their anonymity. The most successful sales organizations use customer feedback to continually improve. As with anything, simply gathering meaningful information without taking action is folly. We recommend using this information to:

o Train your team on areas of deficiency.
o Coach to buyer requirements, wants, needs, fears, and challenges.

- Recognize positive behavior that led to wins. Reward it. And more importantly, document it so that the behavior is repeatable.
- Improve your content and messaging to meet customer requirements.
- Be more relevant when a sales professional isn't present; i.e. improving the content to which the prospect or customer is exposed.

2 - We also recommend getting an external opinion from a dispassionate third-party firm. All of us have "blind spots." Sometimes these blind spots can result in *the curse of knowledge,* in which the sales executive is confident, but possesses a trait of many successful leaders: Self-Awareness. These leaders know that they don't know everything. The typical executive has deep domain knowledge which inhibits his or her ability to look at problems with an unbiased perspective. This is where a third-party, such as Polaris, may be helpful in analyzing your business. Find someone you trust to give you a second opinion. This could be a peer in a similar situation. It could be a 3rd party consulting company. It might be a mentor. Bounce ideas off someone that has been there before.

3- Expand your professional network – and expand it strategically. Don't just connect with your buddy from college. The goal is to get access to your buyers. Once you have access, the marketing process begins. Don't wait for your team to stumble across your top prospect list. Help them get introductions. This may require some research on where your buyers spend time:

a. Start by expanding your LinkedIn network – connect with customers, peers, industry experts and prospects. Initially, don't ask for anything. Instead, seek to give and become a resource to those in your network. Think about who you can introduce a prospect to. Can you introduce them to a potential customer? Do you know someone that has dealt with issues similar to those that they are facing? "Giving" builds *social debt* that will be repaid.

Imagine feeding ideal buyers to your team that feel they owe a debt to your firm!

b. Build your dream customer list – map out all the buyers you want to be introduced to in each account. Look for ways to connect. Can any of your current customers introduce you? Do you have LinkedIn connections in common?

c. Find out where your dream customers spend time – attend trade association events. Sign up for some of the same webinars that they join.

4 - The highest echelon of sales professionals or their managers and other leaders will take the defined steps and will always have a "Call to Action."

a. Develop your own Win/Loss form, or contact Polaris to request a copy of ours. Begin incorporating customer and prospect feedback into an actionable framework.

b. Implement the feedback– get really good at capturing customer feedback. Make it second nature.

c. Teach your team how to do the same – the best way to hold yourself accountable is to teach someone else. You want an unbiased, dispassionate third-party to perform Win/Loss interviews. But you can teach your team to ask for feedback when they lose deals.

5 Keys to Empowering Your Sales Team

An astronomical observation shows that the very brightest stars burn and die out the fastest. What's true in the celestial arena is true down here on Earth, too. Because you're a leader of a business, don't make the mistake of trying to shine the brightest to attain success. Dim your presence in the sales process to empower your sales team, and you might be surprised at how well you can manage the team you've built.

Divide and Conquer

Since you're the leader, your prowess is already established because of what you've done to earn that title. As the leader, it's not your job to lead in sales; it's your job to lead the sales team.

Getting out of your own way and pushing your team to make the sales will 1) allow you to take an omniscient view of the whole process to tweak things as needed, and 2) enable your team members to gain confidence and rapport with their clients so business can stay rolling with everyone involved.

If you're the only person clients want to talk to, what is everybody else doing? Be the manager. You could take on the bigger clients' requests, but for everyday sales endeavors, let your team members do their jobs. You will make more money and have less stress if you push your ego aside and empower others to perform.

Empowering Others

What does empowering others do for your unit? It gives others a sense of power and affirmation. This energetic dynamic can help the group reach new heights because people will want to rise to every occasion where they are expected to take the lead on their own.

Give a sales professional an opportunity to prove himself or herself, and you'll get his best work because he knows he's in the spotlight in that moment. Become your team members' biggest fan, and they'll not only perform for their clients and themselves, but they'll perform for you, too.

Exhaustion Is a Self-Inflicted Wound

Fatigue will set in for any job that's worthwhile. Perpetual exhaustion, however, is a different beast that you, as a leader, can control. If you feel constantly overwhelmed and stressed out because of the insane amount of work you have, then it's probably no one's fault but your own.

If you constantly feel the need to shine brighter than others, the people on your team will start to feel like your assistants instead of your partners. That's something very dangerous to a sales team because once people start feeling used or unincorporated, resentment sets in that can be detrimental to a business that demands cohesion.

Step Out of the Spotlight and Into Action

Now is the best time to start this transition. Here are five ways you can begin the process and motivate your sales team to jump on board:

1. Know what they want. This is the easiest step because it's cut-and-dried. Ask your team members what they want as their own goals. What roles do they want to play on the team? The answers are easily defined; they know what they are looking for, so flesh out tangible goals and begin the transition together.

2. Be their biggest fan. No matter what your team members' goals are, encourage them! Most people have lofty goals and the ambition to pursue them, but some are held back by a lack of support. As the sales leader, it is your responsibility to serve as the support system they need to realize their goals.

3. Create a plan. The first two steps are only prerequisites to the strategies you must put in place if you want to succeed. Create a timeline to visualize where you want to be in the next six months to a year, and stick to that plan. Having a strategy in place breeds enthusiasm and gives the entire team a vision of where it could be in the future.

4. Hold them accountable. If your team isn't excelling, you must be the one to accelerate its efforts forward. It's not about giving your team members a guilt trip for letting everyone down; it's about proving to them that they're better than the results show. It's about leading people through the bad times and giving them a second wind to realize their ultimate goals.

5. Bring out their best. The accountability aspect is key when results are lagging, but after exposing your team members' weaknesses, you must ignite their strengths. What are their natural talents that you can enhance? What is holding them back that you can help them overcome? Ask yourself what you can do to help them, and then make it happen.

5 Keys to Innovation Success

While at the consulting firm McKinsey & Company, two researchers worked on a project to improve the firm's own ability to generate ideas. They looked at extremely successful businesses: ones that had either reshaped the entire industry or went from zero to a billion dollars in sales in under six years.

In 42 of the 43 businesses they found that "the founder had asked a single question at the outset — or could have asked a certain question — that would have led you to same idea."

Arm & Hammer Baking Soda is one of the model companies. Until the early 1970s, Arm & Hammer was mostly used for baking. Then the company asked, "Who uses our product in surprisingly large quantities and how can we get more people to use our product that way?" When the company noticed a small number of customers using its product to deodorize refrigerators or to aid in washing clothes, it created a campaign to encourage customers to expand their use of baking soda. Today, the majority of its business comes from these other uses.

The researchers deduced a set of guidelines based on such examples that can help other businesses come up with similarly groundbreaking ideas:

- **Acknowledge your constraints upfront.** Brainstorming often fails because it is too unfocused, scattering participants' creative energy. In the real world, constraints exist.
- **Ask focused questions.** A good question forces you to look at a problem from a different angle. Instead of asking an overly broad question such as "How can we increase profits?" ask a more focused question like, "What's the biggest hassle customers face when using products/services in our category, and how could we eliminate that hassle (in ways that others haven't done already)?"
- **Don't assume that you (or your staff) can't come up with creative ideas.** The stereotype that some people are analytical and others are creative, but that people can't be both, is not true.

These are complementary forces that work together to produce better ideas. One helps you evaluate whether ideas are good or bad, the other gives you perspective to help identify a new category of ideas.

- **The "brainsteering" concept encompasses a wide variety of activities**. Research shows that voice-of-the-customer research is a very productive and effective source of major ideas and "big concepts." Here the goal is to uncover the customer's or user's <u>unspoken</u> and <u>unmet</u> needs, to understand their problems and "points of pain", and to conceive winning solutions. Ethnography, lead user analysis, and depth visitation programs are effective here. But there are many other methods – strategic approaches, technology developments, internal ideation – which are effective as well.
- **Having the right climate, culture, organization (team-based) and leadership for innovation** – the people side, which is perhaps the most difficult to achieve.

Your Performance Reviews are Done Wrong!
<u>**5 Tips for Improving Performance and Enhancing Relationships**</u>

Up Your Frequency

There are a litany of reasons managers give for why they don't provide feedback more frequently. They don't have the time. They think that empowering people means letting them figure everything out for themselves, including what they're doing right and wrong. Some feel they aren't any good at coaching, while others are conflict avoidant or afraid of spoiling the collegial work culture. "All of these things contribute to managers being either unwilling or unable to engage in sufficiently detailed and consistent dialogue with their people," says an expert in the field.

The problem is that when conversations providing feedback happen infrequently, they have a tendency to cause more harm than good. Use the analogy of working out: If you go out and try to do a five-mile run without working out regularly, that's when injuries occur. Part of why the ongoing dialogue works so well is it lowers the stakes in each of the conversations. Think about what happens in the 6- and 12-month reviews. You're talking to people about stuff they did 6 or 12 months ago, for one thing. And their reaction is, "Wow, I wish you would have told me that at the time."

Not that performance reviews should be tossed out altogether. But instead of bringing new feedback to the table, they should summarize the ongoing dialogue and how the employee can take his performance to the next level. Big picture stuff. Meanwhile, the ongoing discussions should provide clear goals, concrete expectations, a timeline, and requirements within which to meet agreed upon goals.

Get Your Motives & Your Facts Straight

Much of the work that goes into providing effective feedback should actually take place well before you sit down with an employee. Having clear intentions for the conversation will help set an appropriate tone, says Joseph Grenny, co-author of *Crucial Conversations: Tools for Talking When Stakes Are High*. If you come from a place of anger or revenge, it will hamper progress. "We know that coming at people with that kind of motivation is going to shut them down," says Grenny. "They're going to get defensive; they're not going to be interested."

Before offering feedback, Grenny suggests asking yourself three questions: What do I want for me? What do I want for the other person? What do I want for the relationship? "The people that are really good at creating a non-defensive, open conversation with people tend to talk to people from a perspective of, 'I care about you and I want you to be able to achieve the results that are important to you, and I want to be able to get my results.' When you are coming from that place, people sense it and it colors the entire conversation."

The other homework you need to do before a feedback session is gather facts so you can provide substantive evidence of the points you want to make. "You need to write down what conclusions you want to share with this person about their performance and what supporting facts you have to dredge up to help illustrate the points you're trying to make," says Grenny. "You have to do that work. If you don't, what you're going to be having is an abusive conversation where you insult somebody without informing them."

Stay On Track

It's important to make sure the feedback sessions stay on track, both in terms of the topic at hand, as well as the emotional balance. "You need to be clear on the points you're trying to make and if people are moving off topic, you've got to be good at bringing it back to the central point," says Grenny.

The emotional aspect of a conversation can be a bit more difficult to negotiate. "Oftentimes, if someone is getting loud or argumentative or defensive we think "Oh boy, they can't handle this," so we start being apologetic and watering down our message, and sugar coating it."

This is the wrong approach. The way to handle defensiveness is not to minimize your message, but to make the person feel safe, says Grenny. So when you sense someone starting to bristle, set aside the feedback for a moment, and show them that you have their best interest at heart. "The first thing you have to say is, 'Look, I want you to know that I want you to win here. I'm not giving you this feedback because I'm trying to tear you down. In fact, I need to talk with you about this because I think you got potential here and I want to make sure you achieve your potential.'"

Create a Candid Culture

Many organizations suffer from a dearth of candor, says Grenny. He suggests creating a culture where most performance issues aren't handled by you as the boss, but by the person's peers. "Let's be honest, in today's world we don't interact with our bosses the way we used to when they were standing there with a clipboard on the factory floor observing us."

Grenny says it's key to empower peers to provide each other with feedback and teach them the skills to do so effectively so performance problems are handled on the spot and between the people with which they occur. "You need to be actively teaching skills they ought to use for delivering feedback and sharing things because people don't come into your organization with these types of soft skills. If leaders aren't fostering the kinds of competencies needed to a create a positive cultural operating system, then what you're getting is the path of least resistance, and that's obfuscating, that's politicking, it's withholding, it's all of that negative stuff that creates cancer."

Feedback as Transparency

To that point, encouraging feedback has its operational benefits, but it also contributes to an overall healthy, open culture. Rand Fishkin, founder of SEO software firm SEOmoz, has a notorious proclivity for transparency. He's blogged about the company's ups and downs: his own performance, and an insider's view of mistakes the company has made. "It's expected when you say that your company believes in transparency, that what you really mean is 'We will write about things we do well and we'll share when we've been successful.' And it's actually far more interesting and far more challenging, but also much more authentic when you write about failure."

Transparency and authenticity have already been written into SEOmoz's core values--which Fishkin takes very seriously--but his outward transparency has also been a good model for internal culture, says Fishkin. "That's definitely something that over the years, I've become conscious of. And it's very refreshing. I think it takes a little while for someone who's new to the company to get into that mode of thinking."

Fishkin continues, "In much of the corporate world, what I hear is that a lot of people have this fear around sharing their insecurities or sharing things that have gone badly. At SEOmoz, we're working very hard to make it the opposite."

5 Tips to Ensuring Success in "Team Selling"

In major sales opportunities sales calls often involve more than two people for varying reasons like the need for multiple areas of technical expertise. So, what might sales management do to maximize performance on a large team sales call? From our experience, some ideas include:

1) Make sure all members of the team really do need to be on the call.

2) When team size is large, divide the call into manageable bits and make sure each team member knows the piece for which they are accountable.

3) Establish one team member to be a Call Manager who introduces the purpose of the call, directs traffic during the call, and summarizes the call at the end.

4) Generate a sense of urgency so team members care more about the total project as much as the individual pieces.

5) Provide feedback regularly about the process of the calls

Winning in major accounts takes a lot of time, effort, and resources. It also takes getting a lot of things right – being effective in large team sales calls is one small piece of that puzzle. But it's one worth getting right!

POLARIS
ADVISORY GROUP

<u>5 Ways to Use "Social Proofs" to Persuade Prospects</u>

I don't know about you, but I am only working halftime: 12 hours a day, seven days a week. I'm busy, you're busy, and our prospects are busy. As a sales professional, sales manager or sales executive, you want the prospective customer to make a decision. But, all too often, the prospective customer laments, "Who has the time to make a choice?"

To help prospects choose you, give them a persuasive mental shortcut. You can gain trust with prospects through a proven persuasive technique known as "social proof."

The principle of social proof is one shortcut we use to determine what is correct. Humans naturally want to find out what other people think is correct. As a rule, we reason we will make fewer mistakes by acting in accord with social evidence than contrary to it.

Marketers know this to be true. This is why television sitcoms have canned laugh tracks and commercials use man-in-the street testimonial interviews. Or why we want restaurant reviews from websites like Yelp or hotel reviews from websites like Trip Advisor.

The reason the social proof is so persuasive is because we are all running on information overload. The ever-accelerating pace and informational crush of modern life will make automated decision making more and more prevalent.

How should you persuade prospects with social proof? The answer is to use testimonials with measurable results. Here are five tips about how to do it:

1) **Interview past clients to obtain testimonial quotes you can use**. Sometimes it's best to get an outside expert like a public relations professional or freelance writer to help you with this. You want to drill down to get measurable results. These include raw numbers (increased sales by $100,000), percentages (improved retention rates to 70 percent, which is triple the industry average) or time (accomplished more in six months than in previous three years).

2) **May I please?** Get permission to use the person's whole name, title and company name. Just saying, "Sally from Kalamazoo" or Bob from "Cucamonga" just doesn't build trust.

3) **If you don't ask, you don't receive.** Ask for testimonial letters on client letterhead that you can reprint and use in proposal packages being given to clients. The more you have to choose from, the better.

4) **Tell me a story.** Ask clients who are willing to be your advocate to record their testimonials. One way to do this easily is to hop on a telephone bridge line and record the call (with their permission, of course). This can then be used as an audio file on your website or turned into a low-cost audio CD that you can give potential prospects.

5) **Be a name-dropper.** Pepper your selling tools, news releases, website blogs, speeches, seminars and presentations with accounts of individuals who have benefited from your products or services. Describe the problem in brief and give a measurable result your firm helped to achieve. It's far more potent to say "…using Acme's solution, we were able to grow our book of business by 500%" than it is to simply say "…using Acme's solution, we were able to increase our business."

6 Keys to Prospecting Success
Why "One Size Doesn't Fit All"

Prospecting can be like trying to find a needle in a haystack.

I recently conducted a webinar for a client on prospecting. Leading up to the webinar, I asked what questions the client had in regards to prospecting so I could tailor the content to their particular challenges. I guess I shouldn't have been surprised when I only got one response. And that is not because they are masters of prospecting. Quite the contrary. It's because they do so little of it and were unsure of what questions to ask. Like most sales people, they were doing little prospecting at all.

While most sales people will tell you that creating conversations is important and must happen to succeed in sales, the dynamics of how it works continues to baffle many. When sales people seek to understand it better they find conflicting advice. Different situations rightly call for different approaches, so some of the experts themselves are confused about what works and what doesn't.

If conflicting advice and lack of understanding is holding you back from prospecting and becoming a great sales person, at Polaris we've attempted to break it down to its most simple steps.

First off, let's take a page from direct marketing and its age-old formula referred to as AIDA. AIDA stands for Attention, Interest, Desire, and Action. Think of prospecting as the process of creating attention and interest—enough interest to win a conversation to explore the subject area more deeply.

The goal of prospecting is to create interest and convert that interest into a conversation.

Note that we didn't say that the goal of prospecting is to find someone currently looking to purchase a particular product or service. For most salespeople, this is not what they (should) want to do, because it doesn't work often enough.

When prospecting you will find people who are already in the **Desire Phase** (someone interested in solving a particular problem or purchasing a known type of product or service) or the **Action Phase** (someone already in the process of searching for a solution to the problem), but if your approach is only to look for these people, then you're in for a number of rude awakenings:

- Find someone who is already looking to buy, and they likely have a front-runner in mind. This front-runner is not you.
- If you don't sell a commodity product or service, it's likely that the buyer isn't considering buying what you offer because she doesn't know much (if anything) about it, let alone how it works, and why it's worthwhile.
- Find someone who has the desire to solve a problem and hasn't yet started looking into how to do it, and you're in luck! But finding these people will be like finding the proverbial needle in the proverbial haystack.

If you are the one who can capture **Attention** and stimulate **Interest** and **Desire**, you will be the front-runner, you will shape the prospect's understanding of the importance of solving a particular problem, and you will be in the position to persuade them into **Action**.

To really be a successful prospector, here are the six keys:

1. **Targeting**

   The foundation that underpins sales prospecting success is the strength of your list and the precision of your targeting. Salespeople often call too low in the organization and try to start a groundswell by working their way up. Reach high to the decision makers. Make sure that your list is clean and ready to go before you start, or you'll find that your day is lost in fits and starts.

2. **Value in Every Touch**

   When you sell, no one wants to hear your capability pitch, your history, or your life story right off the bat. They're looking to find out how their lives can be enriched by working with you.

   When you think about providing value, don't just think about the value you will eventually provide when they buy from you. Think about the value they'll get just from speaking with you. Eventually you'll sell your company, your offering, and yourself. At first, sell the idea that the prospects' time will be well-spent if they elect to speak with you.

3. **The Right Offer**

Your ultimate offer might be a particular type of software, technical instrument, building materials, financial product, operations plan, or marketing tactic. But the interim offers—the offers you make and they accept *before* they buy from you—must be crafted with the utmost care.

4. **No Tricks**

Plenty of business success awaits you with your high-integrity approach. There is no need to use tricks, bend the truth, or cut corners to generate an initial conversation. Anything that you wouldn't feel comfortable telling your children about when you tuck them in bed at night, leave out of your sales prospecting techniques.

5. **Multiple Touches**

It takes more attempts than most people think to get through to top prospects. It can often take seven, eight, nine, or more touches to get through to someone. That number goes up and down— across different industries and when you reach out to different titles. What's always true though is that it takes more attempts to get through to your targets than you think.

6. **Variety of Touches**

Cold calling works well alone, but it works even better with mail (yes, we are talking snail mail here) and e-mail touches. Use a variety of touches to reach out and warm up your prospects - and make sure each touch has value in and of itself (see #2).

© P o l a r i s A d v i s o r y G r o u p , L L C

6 Tips to Giving a Stupendous Presentation

It may have been a few years since you graduated from B-school. Since then, you've done dozens, maybe hundreds, of formal and informal presentations to employees, investors, managers, clients, and others.

Now ask yourself, "How effective am I really? Do my presentations motivate others to action? Are they inspiring?"

If it's been a while since someone congratulated you for a stupendous presentation, perhaps you could use a mini refresher in presentation pointers. It never hurts to revisit some fundamentals.

Here are six of them:

1. **Identify the "why" of the presentation.** Many presentations aren't appropriate for the timing or for the material. And often, one is asked to present to someone but really isn't sure of why or what the desired outcome should be. Why now? What's the significance of this timing? Why this audience? What does the listener hope to know, and why? Why are you presenting this information at this time? Outline what you hope to accomplish before you begin.

2. **Identify the "who."** Connect with your audience. What do you know about this audience? What matters to them? What do they hope to get out of this? What do they know, and not know? It's a common mistake for the presenter to work hard on the message but then fail to modify it for this audience. In a one-on-one presentation, you can ask

the listener to answer some questions first, such as, "What's most important to you?" You may also say something like, "Before we start, there are six key items I've been asked to focus on in this presentation. Has anything changed, or do you have anything to add?"

3. **Chunk the information.** Many of us are guilty of trying to pack information and data into one continuous flow. Instead, look at your information and ask yourself, "What are the themes?" Organize the information into a handful of topics. Then categorize the information under each heading. When you present, your audience will be better able to take in the details after you give them an overview of the segments — as in, "I have three key points." Open and close each section so the listener knows which information they're hearing.

4. **Make it matter; provide context.** How can you bring your information around to address the needs of this audience at this time? Why does this matter to them?

   Don't leave it up to chance that the listener will understand why this information matters. Keep asking yourself, "So what?" Why does this concern your audience, why does it help them, why might they need to know it? Make it clear. If you can't give context and clarify the meaning of what you're presenting, then that information shouldn't be there.

5. **Match behavioral style.** Particularly in one-on-one meetings and in small groups, a presenter needs to listen and watch for others' preferred style before he or she engages. Style is our tone of voice, our pace, the words we use and our body language. What's the communication style of your audience? How can you shift your approach to make the person or audience feel most comfortable? Excellent presenters use different tones, styles and communication in response to different audiences.

6. **Bring closure.** Circle your audience back around to what you started out with as the objective. What did you want to happen — sharing of information, need for a decision on some data, the "close" of a sales process? This is

where you ensure that the listeners received what they need. Before you leave the presentation, reconfirm the desired outcome: "As a result of this presentation, I wanted you to understand three things" — then list them. "Next step, I've asked each member of this audience to …" Vote? Give me a business card? Buy my product? Be sure when you end the interaction, whether one on one or in a group, that you've confirmed what you hope will happen next.

Using these six keys to presenting will enable you to stand out and be more confident and effective. A little refresher course may be all you really needed.

POLARIS

ADVISORY GROUP

<u>**6 Tools to Inspire High Performance by Your Sales Team**</u>

What drives sales professionals to perform? While money is one motivator, it's not the only thing. In fact, most high-performing salespeople achieve their best results because they are motivated by accomplishment and recognition first, and money second.

It's common, but problematic, for managers to assume everyone is motivated by the same thing. The key to creating a top-performing team is finding the unique factors that drive your sellers. Here are six ways to do this:

1. Ask your sales professionals how they would like to be rewarded if you have a) no money to spend, b) if you have $100, c) if you have $1000, or d) if you have unlimited dollars. This seems obvious, and yet is rarely done. Try it and you'll likely find a pattern that is useful in creating a personalized motivation plan. For example, a new mom (or dad) chose "time off" as her reward regardless of the dollar investment. Others, such as a single man in his 30s, wanted a ski trip and a big screen TV, while a 55-year-old empty nester asked for a lease on a Porsche.

2. Have sellers set their own goals. After the quota is set, work with your sales professionals to develop their own detailed target lists, which could include plans on how to accomplish their targets, stretch goals for reaching beyond their targets, or specific goals per customer on how many more products and services you want them to purchase in a specific time frame.

3. Protect your team. Make sure the entire company knows not to bother your team or create non-revenue-generating meetings or activities during the last week of the month or the last week of the quarter. Your teams will stay motivated if they know you've "got their back" and are looking out for them and protecting their crucial selling time.

4. Reward your team verbally or with an e-mail when deals are won or saved, or when reps hit their quota. Make sure the progress your team makes is publicly acknowledged, and that you celebrate both big successes and small victories.

5. Separate the manager from selling. If you have your own territory as a sales leader, you are competing against your reps. When forced to do both, a sales manager will always sell first and manage later. If they have time. Managers that sell ignore their team, and worse, face the accusation that they are "taking the best leads," and "managing the best territories." Nothing demoralizes a team faster than having a player/coach/manager in place. If your management is pushing this on you, push back. And push back hard with the facts outlined here.

6. Have a commission plan that rewards the team for the behaviors you want. When setting this plan, here are three things to consider:

- **Keep it simple.** The more complex the compensation plan, the easier it is to misunderstand. When the team misunderstands the compensation plan, they assume the company is looking for excuses not to pay them. Sales professionals can often be skeptics (and frequently with good cause).

- **Make sure everybody knows and understands the rules.** Introduce the plan a couple of weeks before you implement it, giving your team a few days to digest its contents. Then hold a group meeting to discuss it. Meet with each salesperson privately to reinforce the plan and address questions and concerns that weren't raised by the group.
- **Encourage team-building to ward off conflict before it starts.** Have competing reps (for instance, inside and outside sales) meet to establish relationships and build trust. The most motivated teams always engage with each other.

Remember that money is just one tool you have at your disposal. Sales professionals who underperform may not respond to a one-size-fits-all strategy, so be sure to ask everyone on your team: What motivates you? And why?

7 Key Drivers to Close the Sales "Strategy-to-Execution" Gap[1]

1. Is there a clear link between the overall organizational strategy and the sales organization's specific sales strategy?

The sales organization's sales strategy must be a direct outgrowth of the overall organization's strategy. The senior sales executives must meet and develop a clear set of their organizational sales goals in complete alignment with the organization's strategy. They must clearly identify not only specific sales goals, but also the priority of each goal.

2. Is the sales strategy known and understood throughout the sales force?

While most organizations have articulated some form of a sales strategy, it has not always been communicated effectively to the rest of the organization. Research has determined that 35 – 40% of organizations do a poor job of communicating the strategy and goals in a way that makes them meaningful and understandable to others in the organization.

For a sales strategy to be understandable, it must be more than an opaque table of projections, forecasts, and numerical estimates. It must be a clear articulation of what the sales force is charged with doing, and communicate the reason accomplishment of that charge is critical to the organization. Often, the "what" is not completely clear, and the "why" is non-existent.

3. Does the sales force (sales managers and sales representatives) have the capabilities required to execute the sales strategy?

This question should move the organization's focus to ground level. Does the sales force have the skills and knowledge to effectively execute and achieve the organization's specific sales strategy? Capabilities within the following three areas should be assessed.

a. Capabilities of salespeople

Most organizations have salespeople who do "all the right things." Research and experience indicate that salespeople dress appropriately; they know their product or service; and they know their customer, the marketplace, and competition.

Most capability gaps occur in interpersonal skills, such as, "ability to develop product/service solutions for different customer needs," "effective management of customer objections and concerns," or "adapting the sales approach to customers' behaviors and personal needs."

The ability to interface with the customer is vital. These people skills often are a major differentiating factor among salespeople. Gaps between current capabilities and those required by salespeople to reach the sales strategy goals call for developmental efforts.

b. Capabilities of first-line sales managers

It is ironic that this group, which research indicates is pivotal in achieving the organization's specific sales strategy goals, is frequently left out of the sales execution equation. Often, the first-line sales manager acts as an administrative arm of more senior management.

Little value is placed on close salesperson coaching skills. Yet, research indicates that this manager's ability to guide and support the salesperson's selling practices is a vital part of ensuring sales success.

Desirable interpersonal coaching capabilities include: "effectively motivating and inspiring salespeople by understanding their needs and aspirations" and "coaching the salesperson on more effective ways to interface with the customer." Even seemingly administrative tasks can require excellent coaching capability.

Examples include "ensuring that salespeople have the necessary resources and tools to maximize selling effectiveness" and "gaining commitment to company directives, programs, and initiatives in order to maximize the achievement of sales strategy goals."

c. Commitment level of senior sales management

The senior executive group must be committed to the success of the field sales force in executing the strategy. The group must make certain that its policies and communications actively support field execution. Without successful execution, efforts are often superficial, incomplete, and do not work. It must "walk the talk." One of the main barriers to turning knowledge into action is the tendency to treat talking about something as equivalent to actually doing something about it.

Senior management must answer questions, such as: "Are sales managers recognized and rewarded for developing and coaching salespeople?" "Is hands-on observation, coaching, and development of salespeople by sales managers given a high priority in a sales manager's job responsibilities?"

"Does the job structure and specified responsibilities for sales managers allow adequate time, attention, and resources for salesperson coaching and development?"

Comparisons of the answers to these questions received from

senior sales executives, as well as salespeople and their sales managers, will uncover whether the groups agree that senior management will support their field sales efforts.

4. Does the sales strategy form the foundation for planning and focusing sales resources at field level?

This is another critical step in executing a sales strategy that is too often not a reality. Effective business plans have three essential roles: first, to state clearly the company's objectives; second, to specify new initiatives, required resources, and expected results; and third, to guide the day-to-day activities of the company toward maximum profitability. In most companies, the first objective is usually met, the second is sometimes met, and the third is often neglected. When this occurs, it causes the sales force to be disconnected from profitability.

Final implementation must always occur at ground level of the sales organization. What happens between sales manager and salesperson and, finally, what happens between salesperson and customer, make or break even well-made plans. In order for sales managers to play this day-to-day role, they must assess and coach individual salespeople in their sales executions with key customers. Goals and expectations must be clear and unambiguous.

These expectations will encourage coaching and dialogue between sales managers and salespeople. This process gains salespeople's commitment to what they need to do to achieve both individual targets and overall sales strategy goals.

This type of leadership and one-on-one planning is of utmost importance. It is what moves the sales force from talk to action. Just as people confuse talk with action and mission statements with reality, they frequently confuse having a plan and doing planning with actually implementing the plan and learning something. There are file cabinets in organizations filled with plans and strategies that remain unimplemented.

5. Do the sales organization's leadership policies and actual practices support the effective execution of mission-critical sales behaviors?

A small sales force may have only one sales manager or head of sales. Larger sales organizations have multiple levels of management spread out geographically, often across continents. Regardless of size, the connection between sales strategy goals and the sales leadership at a first-line level is of utmost importance.

One must ensure that sales strategy goals, roles, expectations, support, and accountability remain aligned and executed as one moves down through levels to the first line. This requires close initial scrutiny and constant monitoring as to whether all levels are "walking the talk." Senior management, particularly, must be open and candid about critiquing its role and responsibilities in setting the tone and modeling accountability for all other levels.

To elaborate, it is the job of first-line sales managers to clarify expectations, provide necessary coaching and management support, and hold salespeople accountable for achieving sales objectives. The next level of sales management must then be doing the exact same thing for first-line sales managers.

They need to know that providing expectations, support, and accountability for their people is a central expectation of their role. In addition, they also need the support of their managers, as well as management accountability.

This alignment of expectations, support, and accountability extends from the sales head, down through all levels of management, to the line salesperson. If at any level expectations, support, or accountability are missing, execution begins to falter and alignment of activities with strategy then becomes problematic. This cascading chain of leadership responsibility is critical for sustaining the clear line of sight and linkage between sales strategy and eventual execution.

6. Do salespeople understand how their sales practices and behaviors make possible the achievement of the organization's sales strategy?

The answer to this question demonstrates the need for sales leadership at all sales management levels, but particularly at the first line. Our research has validated that clarity in expectations is essential to performing well in any endeavor.

Unfortunately, clarity is often lacking. In a 2005 study, performers were asked what one additional management action would be most helpful to them in improving their personal performance.

The most often mentioned item was "A clear understanding of what is expected of me." In a similar fashion, research on performance expectations has established that while first-line managers claim that they give clear, set performance expectations 84% of the time, their direct reports say this occurs only 39% of the time — a huge gap.

This gap occurs for several reasons. At least two are related to sales cultures. First, since most salespeople have a sales quota for a given period, it's easy to assume that "everyone knows what's expected of them."

Of course, the problem is that the sales quota does not specify what prospects should be pursued, which accounts should be selected, what criteria should be used for qualifying prospects, what products/services should be emphasized, etc. These are the expectations that really align activity with strategy goals, not simply quotas.

Two measures help to ensure that expectations are in line with the defined organizational sales strategy. First, clarity is achieved by using the SMART criteria for goal setting. Most organizations are familiar with these. They specify that expectations should be specific, measurable, achievable, realistic, and timely. Second, by using an online performance support system in which salespeople can enter goals and action plans, both sales manager and salesperson can jointly track and monitor progress towards goal achievement.

Performance research has also confirmed that expectations which are defined and tracked are far more likely to be achieved. This moves us closer to execution of a successful sales strategy.9 Discussion of a computer-based goal tracking system brings us to the final critical link in our system, ensuring outcomes.

7. Is there a mechanism in place to track progress towards sales goals that will ensure accountability for, and adherence to, sales practices and behaviors?

Once we have clarified what sales practices and behaviors are critical to achieving the desired sales results, a mechanism is needed to ensure that they are being effectively executed across the sales force.

Fortunately, the same performance system used for setting expectations and planning actions can also be used to track goal progress. This final element in our system can be used in an ongoing way to ensure that salespeople and sales managers do what they say they will do with key, high-potential customers.

In Conclusion:

The path from setting sales strategy goals to obtaining measurable sales results requires support; commitment; accountability; execution; and, most of all, leadership. The majority of leadership and execution behaviors described call for perspiration, not inspiration.

The task of providing a compelling and strategic sales strategy, of gaining commitment to it, and of keeping people engaged as they move toward achievement is not esoteric. It does require discipline and effort. The payoff, however, can be substantial.

Polaris Advisory Group works with organizations to ensure that their sales strategies support and contribute to the attainment of the overall organization objectives. Our model, "Purposeful Selling," is designed for senior sales professionals and is intended to elevate their status to that of "Trusted Advisor" to their clients.

We believe that any organization can achieve a significant competitive advantage by keeping a laser-like focus on implementing the common sense steps described in this article.

[1] Attribution and appreciation is acknowledged to Blessing & White, Harvard Business School Working Knowledge Newsletter, Harvard Business School Press, J. Pfeiffer and R. Sutton, Vignettes in Training, Psychological Associates, Inc., and William Beane.

POLARIS
ADVISORY GROUP

7 Keys to Developing a Successful Business Plan

At Polaris Advisory Group, we believe that – regardless of the size of your business – having a documented Business Plan is critical. Our process in working with clients to develop a successful business plan incorporates these seven key objectives:

- The Business Plan provides a process for thinking through every aspect of your business. This can keep you from making serious mistakes.

- It helps you understand how much money is needed and when.

- A good Business Plan provides support for achieving financing (banks and others require a business plan before they will grant you a loan).

- A well-thought-out Business Plan helps you to understand and plan for competition so you can compete successfully. What are your exposures? What are your competitors' weaknesses? What can you and should you do to exploit them?

- Your Business Plan should incorporate your "Unique Value Proposition" – what is it about your business that uniquely positions you in the marketplace?

- The Business Plan begins with your organization's high-level goals and objectives, considers your exposures and includes plans to mitigate them and drills down to a task level for each department: what needs to be done, by whom and by when. This provides you with a tool to gauge your progress on a regular basis.

- It provides you with a road map that you can use to run your business. A solid plan helps you to keep your business under control and guides you when you need to make detours, change directions, or change the speed at which you start and operate your business. It is re-visited often and on a regular schedule. It is a dynamic document.

We've found that a planning session to develop your Business Plan, facilitated by an dispassionate third-party, is the best way to develop a sound plan and to keep your business's management team on track in its development. We'd welcome the opportunity to work with your firm in developing your Business Plan.

"Lean Into Your Fears"

One of our firm's most rewarding practice areas is Executive and Leadership Coaching. Often, we learn as much as our clients. And one of the key findings from having completed dozens of engagements with executives and leaders who seek to hone their skills is that many of those with whom we work operate from a position of fear. This is not to say that these leaders are cowering in a corner or are afraid to make a decision. Indeed, these leaders wouldn't be in their positions if they didn't exhibit courage on their way up "up the ranks."

The type of fear we see is far more subtle. And often, our clients aren't even aware of it on a conscious level. But it can affect the executive's subordinates -- and their subordinates -- until there exists a "culture of fear" at all levels of the organization.

Frequently, as we "un-pack" the root causes of these fears in conversations with executives within the organization, we learn that these fears are generally based on assumptions and the presumed negative consequences of taking action. When the executives realize there isn't truth to what's driving their fear, they can move ahead and take action on those things that have a profound impact on their ability to lead in the best way.

Fear is a big (negative) driver in many organizations. It lurks quietly behind other emotions, and unless the executives are vigilant, it can stifle their ability to lead as well as they're capable. Because so many of the things that cause fear at work don't "shout out" until they're noticed, they may be overlooked until it's too late. When fear is overlooked or dismissed it can often snowball into failure for a leader. This is entirely avoidable and needn't happen. But the executive needs to be aware of these fears and not treat them dismissively.

If the executive senses personal resistance, reluctance, or even anger about taking action – *lean into* these emotions! Consider what the cost is to the executive personally and to the organization if they prevent the executive from taking action. We believe that the executive or leader needs to ask a series of questions to overcome these fears:

- Is it fear that I feel?
- What is driving my fear?
- What assumptions am I making about what might occur if I take action? Are they true?
- How might I overcome my fear?
- What's the worst that could happen if I take action?
- What's the best that could happen if I take action?

We know from our work in this area that, at least with the clients to whom we've been exposed, that they genuinely want to improve their leadership skills – or else we wouldn't be engaged in the first place. And, as a result, we know that the critical question – in addition to the six cited previously – that needs examination and to be answered is a simple one:

- Is taking this action the "right thing" to do?

For leaders who have a solid value system in place and can answer "yes" to this last question, fear becomes a non-issue. Almost miraculously, the executive is called to "lean into that fear" in order to do what is right and to take the necessary action for the greater good.

"Is it the right thing to do?" is THE question to ask when we realize that fear prevents us from taking action.

Whenever we feel resistance, reluctance or anger, we should ask this set of questions, with a focus on the final one. Many executives and leaders do this intuitively, which is why they're in the positions that they are. And ultimately, answering these

simple questions will transform the leader's fear into courage –
to the benefit of not just the leader, but the entire organization.

7 Steps to a Perfect Cold Call

Firstly, we should acknowledge that there's a vast difference of opinion, among experts and sales pros alike, about the effectiveness of cold-calling.

Many sales experts think cold-calling is a waste of time and prefer other forms of generating leads. Others see cold-calling as a last resort, while still others see it as a mainspring of any effective sales process.

Let's assume that the objective of the cold-call is to get an appointment and not to sell something over the phone. By definition, this implies that our cold-calling efforts are going to lead – we hope – to a large ticket sale. Here are some keys:

Research a list of prospects. Before making your calls, research your prospects. Look for prospects who have a similar profile to those who have bought from the past. They'll be easier to sell. Next to each prospect, note any of your current customers in the prospect's industry, region, job classification, or anything else that might help you to position your offering. Don't spend a lot of time on this, just find out enough so that you can pitch using terms that the prospect can understand.

Build your script. Once you know whom you're going to call, focus on what you're going to say. Write a brief script (no more than three or four sentences) that introduces who you are, what you do, and what you provide. An effective script asks for the appointment early. Please note that the purpose of the script is NOT to communicate substantive information about your offering. Instead, the purpose of the phone call is to win the right to actually sell to the prospect.

Anticipate objections. Each time one of them materializes, you'll need to handle them appropriately... and then ask for the appointment. Most objections are common to all sales situations, so you should have little or no trouble listing them out. The trick here is to practice handling objections until the response is automatic. Note: the most important part of handling the objection is asking for the appointment.

Get positive and get calling. Attitude is everything. If your offering has value to the customer, you're doing the prospect a favor by giving him or her the opportunity to meet with you. Therefore, have confidence in your ability to provide value. That confidence not only helps you communicate more effectively, it provides the motivation that will drive you to actually sit down and start making the cold calls.

Leave a message (if necessary). If you end up in the contact's voice-mail system, don't despair. Leave a very brief message based upon your calling script. However, rather than setting a time for an appointment, say that you'll be calling back on a certain date and time, but would appreciate a callback. The next time you call, ask the admin if the contact is in. If not, tell the admin that you've been trying to connect with the contact and would like to know when would be a good time to call.

Handle the objections. Once you've got the contact on the line, execute the script. Don't read it! Put it into your own words, with enthusiasm. In almost every case, you will get at least one, and probably more, objections. Since you've anticipated these objections, you should respond to them as necessary and then ask for the appointment again. If you receive more than 3 objections, it's fair to assume that the prospect is not going to meet with you, so thank the prospect and politely end the call.

Repeat the process on a daily basis. if you're determined to excel, commit to an hour a day attempting to achieve two appointments. If it takes fifteen minutes to get the two appointments, then you can quit early. Practice this regularly and, according to Andrea, you'll very quickly have a calendar full of qualified prospects.

8 Habits of Remarkably Successful Executives

1. They don't create back-up plans.

Back-up plans can help you sleep easier at night. Back-up plans can also create an easy out when times get tough.

You'll work a lot harder and a lot longer if your primary plan simply has to work because there is no other option. Total commitment-- without a safety net--will spur you to work harder than you ever imagined possible.

If somehow the worst does happen (and the "worst" is never as bad as you think) trust that you will find a way to rebound. As long as you keep working hard and keep learning from your mistakes, you always will.

2. They do the work...

You can be good with a little effort. You can be really good with a little more effort.

But you can't be great--at anything--unless you put in an incredible amount of focused effort.

Scratch the surface of any person with rare skills and you'll find a person who has put thousands of hours of effort into developing those skills.

There are no shortcuts. There are no overnight successes. Everyone has heard about the 10,000 hours principle but no one follows it... except remarkably successful people.

So start doing the work now. Time is wasting.

3. ...and they work a *lot* more.

Every extremely successful executive I know (personally) works more hours than the average person--*a lot more*. They have long lists of things they want to get done. So they have to put in lots of time.

Better yet, they *want* to put in lots of time.

If you don't embrace a workload others would consider crazy then your goal doesn't mean that much to you--or it's not particularly difficult to achieve. Either way you won't be remarkably successful.

4. They avoid the crowds.

Conventional wisdom yields conventional results. Joining the crowd-- no matter how trendy the crowd or "hot" the opportunity--is a recipe for mediocrity.

Remarkably successful people habitually do what other people won't do. They go where others won't go because there's a lot less competition and a much greater chance for success.

5. They start at the end...

Average success is often based on setting average goals.

Decide what you really want: to be the best, the fastest, the cheapest, the biggest, whatever. Aim for the ultimate. Decide where you want to end up. *That* is your goal.

Then you can work backwards and lay out every step along the way.

Never start small where goals are concerned. You'll make better decisions--and find it much easier to work a lot harder--when your ultimate goal is ultimate success.

6. ... and they don't stop there.

Achieving a goal--no matter how huge--isn't the finish line for highly successful people. Achieving one huge goal just creates a launching pad for achieving another huge goal.

The process of becoming remarkably successful in one field will give you the skills and network to be remarkably successful in many other fields.

Remarkably successful people don't try to win just one race. They expect and plan to win a number of subsequent races.

7. They sell.

In a survey of business owners and CEOs in which they were asked to name the one skill they felt contributed the most to their success, the most common response given was "the ability to sell."

Keep in mind that selling isn't manipulating, pressuring, or cajoling. Selling is explaining the logic and benefits of a decision or position. Selling is convincing other people to work with you. Selling is overcoming objections and roadblocks.

Selling is the foundation of business and personal success: knowing how to negotiate, to deal with "no," to maintain confidence and self-esteem in the face of rejection, to communicate effectively with a wide range of people, to build long-term relationships...

When you truly believe in your idea, or your company, or yourself then you don't need to have a huge ego or a huge personality. You don't need to "sell." You just need to communicate.

8. They are never too proud.

To admit they made a mistake. To say they are sorry. To have big dreams. To admit they owe their success to others. To poke fun at themselves. To ask for help.

To fail.

And to try again.

The 8 Most Common Reasons That Sales Teams Lose

We've conducted many Win/Loss Reports on behalf of clients, and over the course of time have interviewed over 1,000 decision-makers as part of these studies. We're always fascinated by how they describe their selection process and why they made their final decision. One of the most interesting parts of the interviews is learning why the competing sales team lost.

There's a natural tendency to assume that the losing salespeople lacked sales prowess that the winning team possessed, that their product was far inferior in some way, or that price was the deciding factor. However, in the overwhelming majority of interviews the evaluators ranked all of the competing salespeople and the feature sets of their products as being roughly equal. This suggests that there are other factors that separate the winner from the losers. Below, you will find these key factors along with a corresponding win-loss interview quote.

Incumbent Advantage. The incumbent vendor has a huge sales cycle advantage and the tendency is for them to win business by default. Based upon our research, the odds of unseating an incumbent vendor is typically about one in five.

"It's a pain to switch vendors. It's a pain to analyze whether you should or not. We naturally prefer working with our existing vendors." —Vice President of Purchasing

Inability to Remove Risk. Customers are never 100 percent sure they are purchasing the right product. Regardless of their confident demeanor, on the inside they are experiencing fear, uncertainty, and doubt. The ability to remove perceived risk plays a key role in determining who wins the deal.

"It sorts itself out pretty fast — those who will and won't make it with us. We are a big company, so there's always a tendency to go with the big players. Who are your proven big-time customers? What resources do you have to get something fixed?" —Chief Operating Officer

C-Level Executive Access. Because every major purchase involves executive level approval at some point, the sales team's goal is to connect with a busy executive and conduct a meaningful face-to-face meeting. However, one of the toughest jobs in all of sales is to penetrate the C-suite, and there is a direct correlation of winning to the number interactions the sales team has with executives during the sales cycle.

"Every salesperson is trying to get into my office and explain how their wonderful products will save me tons of money. Very few do because most don't understand what it takes to sit across the table from me." —Chief Executive Officer

Business Solution Focus. A common interview theme is that both the winning and losing sales teams knew their products very well. However, winners were better able to prove their value as a business partner who had the expertise to solve the customer's problem.

"What's wrong with salespeople is they're typically selling a product. I don't need a product unless it solves one of my business problems." — President

Ineffective Messaging.

Successful communication is the cornerstone of all sales. Winners have the ability to tailor compelling messages that resonate with the various evaluators across the organization and up and down the chain of command.

"We are a skeptical group, and they lost the deal during their presentation. They said they were different and much better than what we have, but they didn't provide enough proof. What they said didn't really apply to us." —Chief Financial Officer

Poor Pre-sales Resources. The complex sales process is typically a team-related sales effort that involves pre-sales product and consulting experts. Losers were often cited as having inferior quality pre-sales resources and equally important, the lack of knowledgeable resources who consistently attended each meeting throughout the sales cycle.

"The vendor we chose has a group of smart, dedicated, customer-oriented people. To a great degree, I don't think their products and services are different from their competitors'. They distinguish themselves with their people." —Vice President of Supply Chain

Lack of an Internal Coach. A clear difference between winners and losers is that the winners developed an "internal coach" within the account. Coaches are evaluators who provide proprietary information about the selection process, status of the competition, and help the sales team determine its best course of action.

"Anytime we had a question, the sales rep attacked it. He would get their people on the phone within a day to answer how we could do something. He listened to what we were trying to do and he knew his resources. He earned our trust so we were much more open with him."
—Chief Information Officer

Out-of-range Pricing. Time after time, interviewees reported they did not pick the least costly option. Savvy evaluators realize there will always be a low bidder. In reality, there is an acceptable price range that the prospect is willing to pay and this can be anywhere from ten to twenty-five percent higher than the lowest proposal (depending upon industry and products being purchased). However, solutions priced outside of this boundary will rarely, if ever, be selected.

"Price is always important but we did not buy the lowest priced solution. There are many other factors including the fit between organizations that render pricing to a secondary factor. With that said, I never want to buy the highest priced solution." —Vice President of Technology. Losing is always hard. Learning you are the loser in the eleventh hour of a deal is a frustrating, humbling, and embarrassing event. If you find yourself in this circumstance, perhaps it's time to honestly ask yourself if any of the factors above were at the root of your loss.

POLARIS
ADVISORY GROUP

8 Tips for Leaders to Unlock Employee Engagement

1. **Give your time.** The greatest gift leaders can give their employees is their undivided attention. Take time to listen. Ask questions. Pay attention to their answers. Find out what they love to do. Uncover their pain points. Follow up to show that you support their success. And don't forget to laugh and joke with them. Ask about their families, hobbies or friends. Yes, business is serious, especially these days, but nothing builds rapport faster than being human with each other. And with rapport, relationships and success can flourish.

2. **Look for their strengths.** See each team member as an individual. What unique skills and abilities do they offer? Are they great coaches to less-experienced teammates? Can they make a spreadsheet sing with insight? Do they have a knack for acting on their feet? Figure out those natural skill-sets and help them develop those skills so they can really shine. Put them in a place where others see these strengths. Stretch them with assignments that draw these skills to new levels. Help them feel great about the progress they are making.

3. **Involve them in the process.** Ask team members for their ideas. Engage small working groups to come up with recommendations for ongoing challenges or needs. Select people to set agendas and lead meetings. Doing this develops your team members for bigger responsibilities and gives them a say in how the team works.

4. **Pick a cause. Get involved.** Even if the idea of taking time from work to volunteer seems odd, time and again, I've seen teams really get engaged when they work together to help others. Doing this under the flag of your company makes them feel good about themselves and the company they work for. Acting in service to others is a great reminder of all that we have to grateful for.

5. **Be honest.** Tell your team members when they are doing great. Tell them how they can improve. Through this you demonstrate respect and you engage in helping them reach their full potential.

6. **Actions speak louder than words.** We have all heard this. So recognize as a leader others are watching you. The good thing is you don't need to be perfect — just authentic. Don't be afraid to acknowledge when you or the organization makes a mistake. By the way, your words have an impact as well. So choose carefully how you speak to your team and others. Create private time for criticism and when you can public time for praise.

7. **Ask for help.** Some of my best relationships at work have grown from asking others for help, when I don't know the answer. Don't be afraid to ask for assistance or input from your team or others. Most of the time they are going to surprise you.

8. **Customize your interactions.** What might work with one employee might frustrate another. Some employees like structured meetings scheduled a week in advance in Outlook. Others are more comfortable with a "drive-by." The key here is to ask your team member how she prefers to interact. Set aside your own biases about formality or informality and work with your team to create agreements on how to ensure great connections.

POLARIS
ADVISORY GROUP

9 Business Books That Will Change Your Life

Great leaders learn every day, and reading great books is the one of the best ways to learn. I've been fortunate enough to read some excellent books over the last fifteen years - books that have inspired me to change the way I see the world, my business, and the opportunities in front of me. In the order in which I've read them, here is a list of nine books which have changed my life. May they change yours as well:

1) *What Color is Your Parachute? A Practical Manual for Job-Hunters and Career Seekers* by Richard Bolles

I read this book when I was 21 years old and didn't know what to do with the rest of my life. It helped me go from a Crunch n Munch vendor at the ballpark to a top salesperson at Radio Disney. Fifteen years later, I have given at least 40 copies away to interns, staff and friends who are searching for their career purpose. It's difficult work - because not only will you read the book, but you'll have to do a lot of exercises and soul searching throughout - but whether you're 21 or 61, you'll emerge with a clearer vision of what you want to do next and where you'll want to work.

2) *Permission Marketing: Turning Strangers Into Friends & Friends Into Customers* by Seth Godin

No author has influenced me more as a marketer, business person and writer than Seth Godin. I could have easily included 9 books just by Godin - *Purple Cow*, *Tribes*, *Linchpin*, *Poke the Box* & his latest, *Icarus Deception* are all amongst my favorites. But

Permission Marketing described social media marketing before it existed. Seth understood push-vs-pull marketing long before others, and this book, published in 1999, is still a must read for anyone in marketing today.

3) *The Tipping Point: How Little Things Can Make a Big Difference* by Malcolm Gladwell

This classic, one of three by Gladwell (*Blink* & *Outliers* are the others), demonstrates how successful products are launched, how ideas spread and how a trend can take off. It's influenced me a great deal, as a <u>word of mouth and social media marketer</u>. And it's an essential read, whether you're in marketing or sales, or just want to become better at getting your ideas to spread.

4) *Good to Great: Why Some Companies Make the Leap - and Others Don't* by Jim Collins

Collins is scientist of great companies - and this is his best work - chock full of case studies and simple yet profound principles like Level 5 Leadership. Even though I read this book when my company was only a handful of employees, it inspired me to want to build something great, and enduring. Whether you work at a large company that has the potential itself to become great and enduring, or you have a vision of a company you'd like to one day build, this is a must-read.

5) *Mastering the Rockefeller Habits: What You Must Do to Increase The Value of Your Growing Firm* by Verne Harnish

It's hard to believe I even had a business before I read this book by the founder of my favorite business group, <u>Entrepreneurs Organization</u>. Verne's <u>1-page strategic plan</u> is now used by both companies I've founded, and thousands of other companies. And our management teams use much of the methodology from this book. What's great is that it's both inspirational and quite practical - an excellent read for any entrepreneur or manager at a small business.

6) *The E-Myth: Why Most Small Businesses Don't Work, and What to Do About It* by Michael Gerber

This is a must read for any small business owner - especially "technical" owners such as lawyers, accountants, florists, restaurateurs, consultants and <u>dentists</u>. Gerber inspires the small business owner to get out of his/her own way, and to build systems and processes that scale and allow the business owner to work "on" the business and not "in" the business.

7) *Built to Sell: Creating a Business That Can Thrive Without You* by John Warrilow

Make no mistake - if you are an owner or leader at a business - this is a great, super valuable read, even if you or your owners have no intention of ever selling the business. The idea isn't to create a business in order to sell it - it's to create a business that has sustaining value beyond you and without you. Warrilow's book is a short, easy story - with powerful, unforgettable lessons - so much so, that after my business partner and I read it, we gave copies to the entire <u>Likeable team</u> to read.

8) *Rework* by Jason Fried and David Heinemeier Hansson

No matter what you do, this easy read will change the way you think about your work. It is so simply written, with small words and big pictures - and yet contains profound wisdom about how to be more productive and successful without being a workaholic or sacrificing anything. I read it in an hour on a plane, and have since shared it with two dozen colleagues, and referred back to it myself at least a dozen times.

9) *The Three Big Questions for a Frantic Family: A Leadership Fable About Restoring Sanity to The Most Important Organization in Your Life* by Patrick Lencioni

Along with Seth Godin, Patrick Lencioni is my favorite business author. I've read and **love** *The Advantage, Getting Naked, The Five Dysfunctions of a Team,* and *The Five Temptations of a*

CEO. But the reason I've selected this one as my favorite, is that, as I've written before here, our ultimate legacy isn't our career, but our family. In this book, Lencioni applies his management consulting methodology and brilliant storytelling ability to the running of a family. It's amazing how little strategy most of us parents apply to the most important organization we've got, our families, and this book helps change all that. Six months after my wife and I read this book, I'm proud to report that our family now has a strategic plan, complete with a mission statement, quarterly objectives, and weekly 10-minute meetings. And it's going GREAT.

Those are my nine favorites- though I've read dozens more I've loved. I've also written a couple of books that I hope have changed a few lives - *Likeable Social Media,* about the role of social media in today's society and how organizations can best leverage it, and, recently, *Likeable Business*, about how to leverage 11 simple principles of customer-centric, staff-centric leadership to succeed in today's social-business world.

POLARIS
ADVISORY GROUP

9 Key Elements of a 360-Degree Feedback Program

Our observations of firms which are successful in implementing 360-degree feedback programs indicate the following commonalities among them. Here's what they do to ensure success:

- They begin by measuring the right skills, relying on empirical research to determine which leadership competencies really make a difference to the performance of their firm, rather than on some senior executive's beliefs about what makes a good manager.
- They take the time to properly explain, both to participants and to the people giving feedback about those participants, why they've going through the exercise and how the data will be used for the participant's development.
- They make certain, and make it known, that there will be no breaches of confidentiality.
- They create a survey that requires just 15 to 20 minutes to complete, to avoid the survey fatigue that tortuously long instruments cause.
- They focus primarily on discovering strengths rather than use the process to uncover deficiencies. Yes, the process sometimes identifies major weaknesses that need to be taken seriously, but in our experience, these have been in the minority of cases.
- They tailor the results to each individual and to his or her position. Everyone doesn't need to be good at the same things.

- They present each person's results in a way that enables them to digest them constructively and use the data to create a personal plan of development. They make the feedback report itself simple to read, presenting data in a graphical format that is easy to absorb.
- They design a final report to help participants see how they compare to those in the top quartile and in the top 10%. This elevates everyone's aspirations. They then follow up with one-on-one coaching to help the participant get there. No one leaves feeling complacent about being slightly above average.
- They include a mini-employee survey that shows managers the impact of their behavior on their subordinates.

POLARIS
ADVISORY GROUP

10 Tips to Lead
<u>Nurturing Success</u>

1. **Start with a goal**: Setting up a lead nurturing program is not a goal. You need to decide what you hope to achieve by setting up a program. Some objectives can include: converting raw sales leads into qualified prospects, identifying key decision-makers, turning dormant accounts into active accounts, etc.
2. **Be consistent:** Pick a timeframe between lead nurturing activities and follow through on it. Don't get distracted and put off these activities. Your prospects will come to expect to hear from you! Don't disappoint them.
3. **Be relevant:** There are certain universal truths which apply to most organizations and which are top-of-mind to every executive: increasing profits…which requires increasing revenues…which requires making more sales…which means generating more leads…which means converting more leads to sales…which means having something such as a "lead nurturing" program. Relevancy is the key factor in generating response. Utilize segmentation and tailor your message for specific lead sources, job functions, industries, product interests and activities.
4. **Mix it up:** Use a combination of White Papers, case studies, press releases, webinars, and other tools as part of your lead nurturing program. Don't be predictable!
5. **Ask the right questions**: In order to create the most effective lead nurturing program, you must evaluate your current lead management processes by asking the right questions. What happens to leads today? Really drill down. It's shocking how many leads never receive any follow-up.
6. **Start small**: Don't get carried away. While marketing automation allows for immediate response, anytime, with multi-step, personalized, dynamic series of email communications, based on demographic and behavioral scoring (deep breath), it doesn't mean you have to implement these processes just yet! Start simple and implement your plan in phases.

7. **Respond to Inbound Leads**: These are the "low-hanging-fruit!" Respond immediately. If you can respond on the weekend, great. You'll be surprised how many people will make an inquiry through your web site over the weekend and are astonished to receive a call-back.

8. **Don't be enamored by marketing technology:** While it certainly has its place, the personal touch is still what most folks react to. Use it.

9. **Make your blog an integral part of the program**: Dump your e-newsletter. Your blog has many more advantages, including: broader reach, interactivity, no editorial calendar, and much more.

10. **Don't forget the thank-you page in your e-mail campaigns:** To most marketers, this page is an afterthought. Make sure you don't miss the opportunity to thank your prospects for their interest in your company and its products!

POLARIS
ADVISORY GROUP

Back to Basics:
<u>15 Fundamentals for Every Sales Professional</u>

While there are many fundamental "basics" that every sales professional knows, we've learned from working with our clients that it's the rare sales professional who adheres to them consistently. Here's our list of 15 -- based on observation. Improving the use of even one can significantly improve results.

1.   The more people talk, the more they like you.

I'm sure you've heard colleagues lament, "He's nice but he just talks too darn much."

But I doubt you've ever heard the opposite: "Darn, she's nice but just listens too much."

Most people, your prospects included, want to be heard and understood before understanding. Effective salespeople are listening 60 percent to 80 percent of the time, depending on the complexity of their offering. They accomplish this by becoming highly skilled at asking the right questions at the right times. View this need as a fundamental rule of communication.

2.   A professional salesperson makes a sales call to be of service to the customer.

If you're making a sales call to meet quota, earn a higher commission, move the "special of the month" or any other reason not arising from your customers' true needs, it's time to check your integrity.

One of the main reasons selling has a negative public perception is too many salespeople sell for their reasons, not their customers' reasons.

3. A qualified prospect has the need, authority and budget to buy.

Ensure the person you're dealing with meets this criterion. If he or she doesn't, find out who does, or you're merely presenting, not selling -- which wastes money and time.

4. No one's born a salesperson.

Similar to every other profession, highly skilled sales professionals have studied and learned their trade. Much as a doctor, attorney or accountant isn't "born," neither is a salesperson.

Abandon this myth and learn your trade. Research reveals that regardless of age, race, gender or experience, a novice salesman with effective sales training can become as successful as his veteran counterpart.

5. What will it do for me?

If the definition of selling could be boiled down to a single sentence or question, this would be it.

Constantly put yourself in your prospects' shoes by asking this question. It will help you focus on their needs and the appropriate corresponding benefits.

6. People don't care how much you know until they know how much you care.

Your prospect must believe that you will do everything possible that's in his or her interest. Without this trust, all the facts, figures and discounts don't mean anything.

Once you gain the prospect's trust, however, you become much more than a supplier -- you become a trusted counselor and partner not easily replaced, despite your competitors' lower price, supposed faster delivery and so on.

7.   People buy emotionally and justify logically.

Contrary to what many salespeople believe, this reality actually works in your favor if you've done a thorough job of helping your prospect buy.

It's imperative that you reinforce your prospect's decision to buy with sound reasons for the purchase. If you allow your prospect to buy a new iMac computer because of the cool color -- without reinforcing the time savings, increased productivity and ease of use -- you might as well keep the shelf space open for the return.

8.   Send thank-you letters.

Does this really need an explanation?

Send thank-you letters to anyone and everyone -- from the receptionist who set the appointment to each person present for your presentation. Short notes take a little time but show a lot of class. This professional courtesy can open an apparently closed opportunity.

9.   Treat every person like the CEO.

It has been said that the true character of a person is revealed in how he or she treats someone who can
do absolutely nothing for him or her. Nowhere is this truer than in selling. This makes good sense, because there's the rare possibility the receptionist will someday become CEO.

More likely, you'll encounter many employees who aren't decision-makers but quickly can become part of the decision-making process. You'd be surprised how many deals salespeople have lost by being rude or elitist.

10.   Always ask whether anything has changed.

This simple question is imperative and helps minimize surprises. Never assume things are where you left off.
Asking this offers you protection and the opportunity to help the customer know you're working in his or her interest. You might discover the budget's been revised, there's a new time frame or, even that your prospect's company has been sold and all deals are off.

11.   Set an objective for every call.

An objective is anything that keeps the sales cycle going -- making a presentation, sending additional information or scheduling a demo. Once the sales cycle halts, it's unlikely you'll get it moving again.

12.   Discuss benefits, not features.

This law has become cliché during the past decade, yet most salespeople still don't apply it.

Consider this: There are more than 1 million half-inch drill bits sold annually, but people don't want half-inch drill bits. They want half-inch holes. Show your prospects the benefits of your product or service.

13.   Sell value, not price.

Surveys reveal that price concerns often are as low as sixth in the order of importance of prospects. However, it's always one of the first objections raised.

If you're continually locked in price wars, you'll rarely win. You must demonstrate the value of your product or service.

14.   Every prospect makes five buying decisions in precise psychological order.

The decisions are about:
-        You, the salesperson, including your integrity and judgment.
-        Your company.
-        Your product or service.
-        Your price.
-        The time to buy.

Know these buying decisions, and tailor your presentation accordingly.

15.   Every prospect buys for one, or more, of six buying motives.

Knowing and appealing to the motives will help motivate your prospect emotionally and logically, moving you closer to a sale. They are:

-        Desire for gain.

-        Fear of loss.

-        Comfort and convenience.

-        Security and protection.

-        Pride of ownership.

-        Emotional satisfaction.

Admittedly, there is nothing in any of these fifteen fundamentals that isn't either common sense or covered in even the most basic sales training course. And yet, after working with literally hundreds

of sales professionals in a very "hands-on" fashion in our Purposeful Selling program, selling fundamentals are often overlooked. They're worthy of management's inspection – and maybe even a "refresher course."

POLARIS
ADVISORY GROUP

15 Tips to Surviving VoiceMail

1. If your goal is to get the phone call returned, don't leave information that would allow the person to make up their mind. Add a call-to-action to your message by providing a key date or something of interest that will encourage the person to return the call. You have to create a reason for them to call you back.
2. Repeat your phone number twice. If the person can't quickly write your number down, you've given them a perfect reason to not call back.
3. Avoid asking ask the person to call you back at a certain time. This provides them with an excuse not to call you.
4. Never state in the message that you will plan to call them back. Again, this only gives the person an excuse to ignore your message.
5. Messages left on a Friday afternoon are the least likely to be returned. For most people, Monday mornings are very busy and, as a result, only high–priority activities will get their immediate attention.
6. Do not leave voicemail messages at odd hours of the night. Most voicemail systems offer a time stamp and the person hearing the message will immediately suspect you really did not want to talk to them.
7. The best hours to leave voicemail messages are from 6:45 AM to 8:00 AM and from 4:30 PM to 6:30 PM. Aggressive people are usually working during these time periods, and the person receiving your message could potentially view you as one.
8. Wisely use time zone changes to make as many calls as possible during the optimal voicemail periods listed in the previous tip.
9. Voicemail messages are an excellent way to introduce yourself to a person. Be personable, yet professional, and link your message to something of interest to the person you are calling (such as another person or event). The recipient may view your message as a waste of time if you have no purpose other than getting your name in front of them.
10. When leaving a message with multiple points, be sure to immediately disclose how many you will be making. This will prevent the recipient from accidentally fast-forwarding or deleting it before it is completely heard.
11. If you can't say it briefly, don't say it at all. Voicemail is not "story time." Leaving a long message is an invitation to have the entire

message skipped. The optimal voicemail message is between 8 and 14 seconds.

12. When leaving your phone number, do not leave your website address as well. This will give the person an opportunity to make a decision about you without calling you back.

13. Leave a "PS" at the end of your message. A "PS" is a very quick, additional piece of information that will connect with the person.

14. Mention the person's first name at least twice in the message, but don't use their last name. Doing so comes across as very impersonal.

15. Refer to a mutual acquaintance in your message as a way of connecting with the recipient. (Caution: Make sure they think positively of that person!).

22 Rules to Live By

1 - Show up for appointments 10 minutes early.

2 - Customers are not always right, but they must be treated as if they are.

3 - When speaking before groups, dress up one level from what the group is wearing; e.g., if they wear shorts and tee shirts, you wear business casual.

4 - Never offer unsolicited advice.

5 - Leave your ego at the door.

6 - Don't waste people's time by sending them jokes or stories via e-mail.

7 - Do not brag by talking about your accomplishments to people who didn't ask you about them.

8 - Be humble.

9 - Proofread your e-mails before you send them.

10 - 80% of your activity should be in your comfort zone, and 20% should be outside it. This keeps you both productive and challenged.

11 - Of the people who opt into your e-list, 90% of those who eventually buy from you will do so within 90 days of subscribing to the list.

12 - The more recently a customer had made a purchase, the more likely he is to do so again.

13 - Old but good advice: under-promise and over-deliver.

14 - Don't give your customers their money's worth. Give them more than their money's worth.

15 - The easiest way to add value to an offer is with a free bonus gift.

16 - The most powerful words in the English language are "free" and "you."

17 - Do unto others as they would have you do unto them.

18 - Spend time with your children while they are still young enough to want you to spend time with them.

19 - Neither a borrower nor a lender be.

20 - Don't be so sure you are right. Perhaps you are not.

21 - Life is short - over in the blink of an eye. So enjoy it now.

22 - Avoid discussing religion or politics with colleagues or customers. There is little to gain from it and much to lose.

POLARIS

ADVISORY GROUP

25 Guerilla Marketing Tactics You Should Be Using

1. **The Calendar** -There are no end of ideas in the calendar for things you can do to find customers and make an impact. Why not recruit some aspiring actors from the local college to put on a little flash mob skit promoting your product or business on National Talk like a Pirate Day.
2. **Sticky Notes** – Another way to use your stamper or even your printer. Sticky notes are noticeable anywhere because people know what they're for: notes. Put these on local business doors, offices, cars, or above mail boxes in apartment complexes and people will take notice.
3. **So many stamps** – Looking for a way to get noticed in the huge pile of advertising mail potential clients get? Send your promo material in a big manila envelope and put 39 – 1 cent stamps on it. Out of 100 envelopes, who's do you think will catch the eye first?
4. **Do Not Disturb** – Heading to a blog expo anytime soon? Get some door hangers printed up with your business information on it and possibly a link to something free on your site. Get the attention of everyone in your market this way, and it's super cheap as well. No one else I know has been doing this so you'll stand out for sure.
5. **Pay it forward** – when you're heading into the movie theater, pay the person's way behind you and tell the cashier to give them your business card. You're not guaranteed that the person will become a client but I bet the word of mouth on that one would be pretty big.
6. **Fake publicity stunt** – you could have people picket your storefront with signs that read "This business is too nice" or "Company X is too good at their job". There are a million fake publicity stunts, use your imagination and I bet it'll work - no matter how weird or out of the box it seems.

7. **Guest blogging** – This is for the bloggers out there, or even the freelance writers. Guest blog on other blogs largely related, or semi-related to your websites niche. Opening other people's eyes to your name and your website is always good promotion, especially if you're an awesome writer. Not to mention networking with other bloggers is great for business as well.

8. **Business Cards** – STOP! Don't skip this one. So many people see this and think you're going to tell them to print cards and hand them out. I'm not! What you do with these cards is head to every library or book store in your city and find the section that relates to your business. Open each and every book and place a business card somewhere in the book. This is great targeted marketing and only costs you a few bucks for the cards and an afternoon of placing the cards.

9. **Bumper Stickers** – These are great because they can go anywhere, not just on your car. Bathroom stalls, street poles, etc. Get creative with where you place them, they can grab people's attention when placed in the right spots.

10. **Temporary Tattoos** – I've seen a post on some guerrilla marketing ideas and they talked about this as well. These tattoos will last for X amount of days and would be perfect for blog expos or other events where tons of people will be. Placing it in a weird place (forehead, neck, full back, foot, etc.) is also a great way to get it noticed. Hey, if people talk about it, that's the whole point right?

11. **Help Home Based Businesses** – most HBB owners try to keep their records hidden from local housing authorities so they're hard to reach. Head over to your local Chamber of Commerce and suggest a HBB committee. They might appoint you head of it (you can even ask to be) and you have a bunch of HBB owners who will come to chat and you can promote to with business cards, flyers, booklets, etc.

12. **"Anything Else?"** – No, the list isn't done yet. These are two words to say right before you exchange money with a client/customer. This will make them think and could open doors to a larger pay day.

13. **Top 10 reasons to choose YOU** – instead of leaving business cards or other promo material at a business or in someone's email box, create a list of the top 10 reasons why the prospect should choose your company. Make them 100% true, humorous and memorable.

© Polaris Advisory Group, LLC

14. **Demonstrations** – got a service business? This is perfect for you. Find a local store that pertains to your services and put on a free demo of your services. Your service involve outdoors? Contact news stations and let them know you'll be offering a BBQ and free service demonstration. The BBQ could get a little costly, but the amount of press and promotion could really pay off.
15. **Print Calendars** – These could be given to each of your clients or left in a store for people to take for free. Print your website address and a little slogan or client testimonial on each month's picture for exposure every day. The people using your calendars will even help you out when they have company over who will see the calendar, especially if the images you use are high end and visually appealing.
16. **Window decals** – get a custom printed window decal on your car with your logo/website and possibly a slogan. Looks professional, and is great for red lights.
17. **On-Hold Messages** – If you don't have an "on-hold" message which promotes your business or special offers – and if you don't rotate this greeting every month, you're missing a tremendous opportunity. Because despite your best efforts, your customers ARE on hold! Don't play music or leave your customers and prospects with silence. Promote your business!
18. **Sponsor an event** – doing this is at most times very inexpensive and also GREAT for publicity, especially if it's a big event. You normally get your logo and business mentioned in all of the event's promo material which is tons of publicity you normally wouldn't get. Be at the event to add extra stickiness to your business name and interact with the guests.
19. **Holiday Greetings** – send emails or snail-mail to your past clients wishing them happy holidays (Christmas, Thanksgiving, New Years). This helps them keep your name/business in their head as well as standing out from the other people they've done business with before.
20. **Charity Donations** – Donate some of the profits you generate every month to charity. Great for promotion in the media and clients to feel like they're helping out the charity by purchasing from you.
21. **Hold a Contest** – This could have 1-10 winners which helps the word-of-mouth promotion everyone needs and wants. You

can gain free press for starting the contest, plus publishing the winners is great for more press coverage.

22. **T-Shirts** – This is great for turning yourself or others into walking billboard. You can give the t-shirts away as prizes which is also another great way of gaining word of mouth promotion. Your t-shirts for the prizes don't need your website address on it. Just give away a great, fashionable shirt and that'll have people eager to tell friends and family where they got it from.

23. **Partnerships** – Do you run a web design business and want to find more potential leads? Try partnering with a web hosting company. Do you have a lawn-care business? Try partnering with a window washing company. Any partnership which benefits both companies is a great idea and a great way at grabbing the attention of new potential clients. Also a great way of giving your business targeted marketing.

24. **Blood Drive** – Host a blood drive, contact newspapers, TV news, radio, etc., and have 1-2 banners up with your website information and also have business cards at the sign-in table. Everyone loves to help their community and giving blood is the easiest way for some people to do that. Putting yourself in the forefront of your city's next blood drive would make your business very visible to a whole range of new potential clients and word-of-mouth advertisers.

25. **Client Appreciation BBQ** – Invite your past clients to a BBQ and let them invite 1-2 friends to come with them. This will help your customers LOVE you even more than they already do, as well as bring some new faces into contact with you as potential clients.

POLARIS
ADVISORY GROUP

Customer Acquisition Management:
<u>Your Key To Success</u>

If you're reading this now, it's because you know—and care—about the importance of great customer relationship management. Congratulations: that's the best way to maintain and grow your business in 2013! But a mistake that many marketers make is in believing that great CRM starts after a customer comes on board.

The reality is that if you're not putting the same care and attention into managing your relationships with *potential* customers as you are with current ones, you may be missing out on a lot of significant opportunities. Management expert Peter Drucker has said that the sole purpose of a business is to create a customer. That may be true, but as businesses have understood and acted on the importance of *retaining* customers, they've tended to take the emphasis off Drucker's "customer creation." A balance of both is necessary for companies and brands alike to be healthy and thriving.

Solid customer acquisition requires, first of all, a financial commitment. A recent study found, surprisingly, that only 34% of companies in its survey had dedicated customer-acquisition budgets, and that, contrary to the assumptions companies make, merely putting a process in place and dedicating a person or persons responsible for acquisition was not enough to create a robust customer acquisition management program. Shifting both money and prioritization to the campaigns was what the researchers found worked.

Another study found (as advocates of customer relationship management have always known) that "acquiring a customer depends on how effectively the organization is able to build a comprehensive relationship with that customer."

This is hardly a surprise, and yet, too often the methods and channels used for new-customer acquisition don't take any CRM principles into account. Lured in by advertising, pay-per-click search marketing, or co-registration campaigns, new customers too often find themselves either overwhelmed by too much contact, or underwhelmed by too little; given too many choices, or too few; and generally not listened to at all.

Not good CRM. Not good Customer Acquisition Management.

CAM—Customer Acquisition Management—should be a total solution streamlined into your company's CRM efforts. It starts with the front end of obtaining a lead, and takes your organization through the process of creating a customer out of that lead, then finally passing the customer on to CRM people so they can move forward with the ongoing customer experience and relationship, just as a runner might pass the baton on to the next person on the team.

It therefore makes absolute sense for CAM and CRM teams to work together to ensure an invisible transition for the new customer, consistency in the way that the company or brand treats that customer, and an overall smooth and positive customer experience. At its best, this experience will engender such loyalty that the customer will eventually become a brand advocate or evangelist, steering other potential customers into the company's CAM and beginning the cycle over again.

Moreover, all of this makes good financial sense. Customer-acquisition strategies can help determine where your firm spends its promotional money, but only if you have a CAM solution that affords you excellent metrics so that you can strategize campaigns and tweak them as results come in. Getting well-qualified leads and nurturing those leads into customers cannot happen if you don't have a way to measure your progress, to see what works and what doesn't, and to change strategies if one isn't working.

The results of these metrics will be different for every company, but the most important factor is being sure that the changes and adjustments you make in response to what you learn are on the back-end ... not in the customer experience area. That needs to be smooth, clear, positive, and consistent.

Making CAM part of your CRM will tell potential customers a great deal about how they can expect to be treated once they—should they!—become your customers. Don't you want to make that the best experience possible?

Key Account Management

Key Account Management is one of the most important changes in selling that has emerged during the past two decades. Key Account Management is a radically different organizational process used by business-to-business suppliers to manage their relationships with strategically-important customers, and it produces measurable business benefits.

Not surprisingly, smart suppliers are keen to implement Key Account Management. But, sadly, many Key Account Management implementations fail and are abandoned. In other cases, suppliers find that they have to make big changes to the Key Account Management programs to get them to function.

The good news is that many of these failures are unnecessary. Key Account Management is a major change, but the chances of success can be dramatically increased by implementing the following seven steps:

Step One: Recognize that Key Account Management is an organizational change, not a sales technique. Key Account Management implementations take years, not months. The companies which have implemented Key Account Management most successfully have been those who thought of it as a change in the way they did business, not as something that is confined to the Sales department. Suppliers who fail in Key Account Management tend to think of it as being an initiative *within* the sales department. This approach is doomed to failure. Key Account Management is a commitment to work differently with certain priority customers and, to fulfill this promise. Other supplier divisions have to understand and support Key Account Management. One obvious example is supply chain management. If a key account is promised priority access to urgent products or services, it is Operations who can provide that, not Sales. Best-practice companies choose to train their operations and supply chain people in Key Account Management as well as their sales people.

Step Two: Get high-level buy-in. An organizational change of this magnitude requires high-level sponsorship, preferably from the executive suite. The best companies, such as Rolls-Royce and Siemens, have high-level sponsors for each of their key accounts. Members of the main board of Siemens, including the CEO, each sponsor a number of key accounts and visit them regularly.

Step Three: Appoint a Key Account Management champion. Once the organization has accepted that it is embarking on a major change, and senior managers understand what Key Account Management is and have bought in to it, the next step is to find someone who is going to champion the Key Account Management program and drive the implementation. Usually, this will be someone high up the organization, and it helps if they report directly to the top management, at least for the duration of the project. That way, Key Account Management gets "a seat at the table" and the champion gets the support they need to make changes. Your Key Account Management champion should be passionate about the program and needs to have good influencing skills and a high energy level. One mid-sized company has two Key Account Management champions who travel the world to 'sell' the message about Key Account Management within the company.

Step Four: Identify your key accounts — carefully. To get the Key Account Management program started, you need to identify some key accounts, and you need to develop an offer that differentiates them from the rest of the customer base. Our advice here is to start small. It is easier to add customers to your Key Account Management program than it is to 'demote' customers once you have told them they are key accounts. Generally, the number of key accounts should be small. Our rule of thumb is somewhere between 5 and 25 key accounts. Even major corporations like Xerox keep the number of true key accounts below 100, and they have far greater resources than most and have been practicing Key Account Management for years. Be clear about what defines a key account and *stick to it*. Don't give in to pressure to add certain customers to your key account program just because they have been customers for a long time, or because they are golfing buddies with the CEO.

Step Five: Appoint and train your Key Account Managers. Many organizations make the mistake of simply moving their best sales people into key account manager roles. That's a mistake, because Key Account Management is about changing the way people work — it is *not* just a sales technique. Converting your best sales people into key account managers might mean you've put a bunch of people into a role they are not really comfortable with, and you have just lost your best sales people as a result. In fact, there are technical people and project managers who can make great Key Account Managers. You need to think about what the role requires (a broad range of skills, including financial, consultative, planning, interpersonal and influencing skills) and then pick the right person for the role. Don't forget to train them: Very few people come into a Key Account Management role with all the skills they need.

Step Six: Set the right metrics. It's been said "that what gets measured gets managed." If you have tasked your Key Account Managers with building long-term relationships with their customers, don't reward them as though they are a glorified sales professional. Traditional sales metrics — such as the amount of time spent with the customer — are irrelevant to Key Account Managers. Many Key Account Managers spend much of their time inside the supplier company, managing things on behalf of the customer. If you pay your key account managers for top line revenue, expect them to focus on short-term sales and not on building longer-term value. The right metric for a key account manager is the lifetime value of their customer (the customer bottom line), not top-line revenues. This is an important point: Key Account Managers typically work on bigger deals for bigger clients. Some of these deals can be big enough that there would be real damage to the supplier company if they went sour. The Key Account Manager should be focused on these opportunities, which are generally longer term in nature, as opposed to quarter-to-quarter top-line performance.

Step Seven: Benchmark and build. Your key account program should not be static over time. Instead, you should keep it refreshed. One way is by moving new key accounts into the program (and occasionally moving former key accounts out if they no longer match up). Another way is by actively seeking best practices, both within and outside your company. Hewlett Packard continually reviews its relationship with customers, reflecting changes in what is important to them. Price Waterhouse Coopers has an internal committee that actively benchmarks its own and other Key Account Management programs in a search for best practice. Remember that even a good program can be better.

Key Account Management can have a profound effect on the performance of the supplier organization. But to get there requires a different way of working. These seven steps will help your organization make the transition to Key Account Management successfully. It won't be easy, but it will be worth it.

What Makes an Effective Executive?
<u>The Polaris Ten-Point Checklist</u>

1. **Know Yourself**: Many people find this an unusual part of being an effective executive. But the effective executive is continually making a self-assessment of his or her weaknesses and seeking out opportunities to improve in these areas through reading, studying or continuing education.
2. **Be the Example**: People believe what they "see," not what they "hear." Be the role model. It's unrealistic to expect your team to "go the extra mile" when their executive is working a "9-to-5" workday. Model the behavior that you want your team to exhibit.
3. **Be Responsible:** Take responsibility for your actions. Search for ways to guide your organization to new heights. And when things go wrong, do not blame others.
4. **Keep Your Team Informed:** The old adage, "knowledge is power," may be true. But that kind of power isn't what will allow you to accomplish things through others. Keep your team informed of good news and bad news.
5. **Over-communicate the Organization's Goals:** Share your vision at every opportunity – in group meetings and in one-on-one meetings. Ask for buy-in. When you get it, your vision becomes a <u>shared</u> vision and everyone is on the same page.
6. **Translate the Vision into Tasks:** Do this with your subordinates and make sure they do it with their subordinates. Ensure that the tasks are clearly understood, reviewed on a regular basis and accomplished. Measure and reward your people on their accomplishment (or failure to accomplish) their tasks.
7. **Empower Your People:** Give them the tools they need to do their jobs and the latitude they need to accomplish their objectives. Develop a sense of accountability, ownership and responsibility in your people.

8. **Be Decisive:** Don't "sit on" decisions. Make them in a sound <u>and</u> timely basis. Use good problem solving, decision-making, and planning tools and let your people know how you arrived at your decision so that the process becomes a learning experience.

9. **Recognize Accomplishment and Failure:** "Praise in public, criticize in private" may be a cliché, but it's shocking how some leaders relish in humiliating their subordinates in public. Don't. But don't avoid confronting failure and turning that failure into a learning opportunity.

10. **Be Caring:** Know your people and look out for their well-being. Know human nature and the importance of sincerely caring for your workers. Send hand-written notes on special occasions. If you know someone on your team has experienced a death in their family, don't be afraid to express your condolences. Better yet, attend the funeral. And if a family member of someone on your team graduates from college as a *Phi Beta Kappa*, send a note and share in their pride.

Brainstorming without "GroupThink"

In two prominent articles published earlier this year in national publications, the concept of brainstorming as introduced in the 1940's by Alex Osborn has been attacked as ineffective and linked to the concept of "Groupthink."

Author Susan Cain points out that the popular view — "Lone geniuses are out. Collaboration is in." — conflicts with research that suggests "people are more creative when they enjoy privacy and freedom from interruption." Some of the most spectacularly creative people in many fields are often introverts who are more comfortable working alone. And in another article the author cites research indicating, "Brainstorming didn't unleash the potential of the group, but rather made each individual less creative."

We have no issue with the importance of the creative individual to generate focused and powerful ideas. Furthermore, we agree that, used improperly, Osborn's process of brainstorming can promote consensus, not collaboration. Suffice it to say, we dislike consensus-based "Groupthink" as much as the next person. Rather, our issue is with the way both articles have attacked Alex Osborn's concept of brainstorming as a powerful collaborative thinking tool. We are strong advocates of collaboration in innovation, and believe that the proper use of brainstorming techniques is a powerful tool in the collaborative approach. Over our many years of experience, we have seen managers effectively use three simple techniques for avoiding "Groupthink" during brainstorming.

Here's how:

1. Assemble a Diverse Team

Build your team with people from different disciplines, cultures and age groups Be sure that some members have necessary and relevant expertise, but that some are naïve about the issue (we call them "WildCards"). We once ran a session for a client team composed of a range of scientists and technologists from Bell Labs where 25 new patent applications were filed — 20 of which came from the participation of a 70 year-old grandmother!

And when you are considering candidates, include different styles of participation and thinking: Explorers (extroverted, inquisitive, comfortable with ambiguity, free-thinking), Developers (creative problem-solvers, sometimes introverted, quieter, but love being given a problem or challenge to solve), and Commercializers (realists, business-minded, practical problem-solvers).

Encourage each type of thinker to play, bring introverts out of their shells and tone down the influence of the extroverts, and leverage their diversity to not only identify a range of possibilities, but to also find ways to make the newer ideas feasible.

2. Focus on Roles: The Client, the Facilitator, and Resources

Somebody has to own the effort. This is the client role. That individual may have a lieutenant, but clientship cannot rest with the full team or even a large subset. That is a sure way to generate "Groupthink." Instead, one person must make the decisions. The team should advise that person and advocate for their positions with passion, but ultimately, the client has to exercise leadership and decision-making — they must pick the final concepts to recommend or implement. This role cannot be delegated.

The client should not be in charge of running the meeting/dialogue. They must keep their heads in the content and not worry about or unduly influence the process. Rather someone else should be in the facilitator role and in charge of the process — facilitating the interaction, drawing out the range of perspectives, managing the brainstorming process non-judgmentally.

Everyone else is in the resource role. They focus on listening, learning, ideating, building on other offers, etc. Resources advocate, but do not decide! If everyone in the room has to agree, then the outcome will be the worst possible aspect of "Groupthink" — a decision in favor of the lowest common denominator, devoid of originality, risk or newness, and only what everyone can envision and agree to.

3. Encourage Passionate Champions

Many people understand and follow the first two rules of brainstorming well. But if they miss this next technique, they miss the real power of collaborative thinking: The power of one. Seems like an oxymoron, doesn't it? It's not. Collaboration helps individuals improve their own thinking and gives them ideas they may not have thought of by themselves. When this happens, brainstorming results in the best of both worlds.

This is where the Passionate Champion plays a key role. In our work, after the brainstorming process, we often open the session up to "Individual

Champions." Anyone, alone or with other people if they need or want help, can pick any idea and develop it further. Even if the idea has already been developed in one direction, a Passionate Champion may see it very differently and develop it in a totally different manner. Or, they can pick an idea that was not advocated by the group or selected by the client, and develop it as they see fit.

In our work, we find that Passionate Champion ideas often account for 50% of those that make it through internal and external vetting, and 20-30% of the ideas that make it into final concepts. What's more, they are often the most breakthrough in terms of truly new, game-changing concepts.

Collaborative innovation involves the genius of the "and" versus the tyranny of the "or." It's not that brainstorming must always turn into "Groupthink" or that introverts or individuals have the best ideas. In good brainstorming, one feeds off the other and the end result is significantly more powerful than either approach alone.

© Polaris Advisory Group, LLC

Major Account "Check-up"

Major accounts are the lifeblood of almost all businesses – lose one and you know it's going to be a bad day. Almost all executives feel are certain vulnerability with respect to their major accounts. This is only natural since they don't have day-to-day visibility into what's going on with the customer. But we believe that if you can pass this "Check-up," you're probably in pretty good shape with your major accounts:

1) Do the trend lines for your major accounts continue to be positive? If you see a blip in a trend line that's historically been "up and to the right," you may want to dig deeper.

2) Do you conduct regular (at least quarterly) reviews with the sales team to set goals for the next review period and review performance against goals for the prior period?

3) Do the Account Plans for your Major Accounts include strategic elements, such as offering to beta test a new or unannounced product with your key customers? Or to develop a product that's unique to that account? Even if it's something as simple as changing the color.

4) Do you personally meet with the senior decision makers, and preferably the CEO, on a regularly scheduled basis? Are these "courtesy calls," or do you have a defined agenda with issues that the customer may be facing with your company?

5) Has your sales professional been assigned to this major account for more than five years? This creates several potential vulnerabilities. You certainly don't want to be in the position of being "held hostage" by the sales professional who has all of the relationships with your major account. Additionally – if a competitor wants to break into your major account, what better way than to hire the sales representative who's already "got the Rolodex" for this customer. The solution: add another rep to the account or make sure that the sales manager becomes more of a "player/coach" for this customer.

6) Is the senior executive from your major account a member of your Customer Advisory Council?

7) Do you provide a higher level of Quality Assurance for products being shipped to your major accounts?

8) Does your executive team align with your customer's executive team? In other words, does your CFO have a relationship with the major account's CFO?

9) Do all departments and groups within your company know who your major accounts are? Do they know to provide a "special" level of care for the employees of your major accounts? Many a relationship has been harmed by a switchboard operator giving a customer executive the "runaround" without knowing the importance of the individual calling or their company.

10) Do you "celebrate" successes with your major accounts? For example, do you "celebrate" the completion of a major project – and not just sales successes? Do you include the customer's staff in these "celebrations?"

11) Have you established a unique toll-free number for each of your major accounts so that your staff can answer the phone with a greeting like "Thank you for calling the 'Customer XYZ' Help Line. How can I serve you?"

How Leaders Spend Their Time Speaks Volumes About What They Value
Organizations React to What They See – Not What They Hear

In our work with senior leaders and asking how they spend their time in their work environment, they report three things more frequently than any other activities.

- Meetings with direct reports.
- Evaluating and analyzing performance data.
- Addressing performance problems.

Certainly, these are important behaviors for senior leaders. But are these the most beneficial activities senior leaders can engage in? We don't think so

Why do senior leaders engage in these activities? Our experience and a significant volume of research tells us that leaders' behaviors are driven by three factors: role models from their past, their social style or personality type, and the organization's culture.

So senior leaders do meetings, analysis of data and address performance problems because they've seen those behaviors role modeled by others, the behaviors fit their social style, and the organizational culture reinforces those activities.

But another, potentially more harmful, issue arises as we look at senior leaders' activities. Their integrity is compromised when their activities — how they spend their time — are inconsistent with what they say is important in their workplace.

For example, senior leaders may say that "people are our most important asset," yet choose not to delegate authority to team members to act independently in the moment. Senior leaders may say that they have an open-door policy yet spend so much time in meetings and problem-solving discussions that their door is closed or they're not in their office when a staffer drops by.

In studies of high performing, values-aligned organizations, a constant is that every senior leader sees his or her role as a "chief culture officer." They allocate time and energy to proactively manage their most important asset — their corporate culture. Their plans, decisions, and actions are easily seen as being aligned with their stated responsibilities to ensure an inspiring workplace.

These leaders take the time to define clear purpose, values, strategy and goals for their organization in today's world, and they help communicate how staff members contribute to those vital elements.

These leaders invest time in observing by wandering around, connecting one-on-one with front-line team leaders and front-line employees and asking how things are going. "What can we do to make your job easier?" is a common question these leaders ask. As they learn about issues that get in the way, they address those gaps with help from those in-the-know, i.e. their frontline team members.

They observe team meetings at all levels of the organization to learn what's working and what's not. They praise progress as well as accomplishment — they know that too often effort is ignored.

They spend less time in meetings with direct reports and more time *observing* their direct reports on the job, helping them praise progress, celebrate traction and value citizenship in their functional groups.

They spend more time helping all leaders and managers learn to effectively address performance issues and misaligned values in their workplace.

On average, these inspiring senior leaders spend 60-70% of their time championing their desired organizational culture – and it pays off. A study of these "culture clients" report gains of 40% in employee engagement, 40% in customer service, and 30% in profits in 18 to 24 months of taking the actions necessary to ensure an aligned effort.

What are your activities saying to your team members about what you value? How often do your senior leaders observe by wandering around and connect with you on how things are going?

9 Negotiation Tactics From Famous CEOs

Everything is negotiable. It's one of those trade secrets every businessperson knows but won't divulge. Because at the end of the day, those who bargain the best are the ones who come out on top. Learning to play the game to your advantage, to disagree without being disagreeable, is more than just a valuable skill—it's key to survival.

To demonstrate several ways to broker a deal, this document describes nine stories from famous CEOs at the negotiation table. While we don't recommend every tactic, you have to admit these moguls know how to wheel and deal their way through business.

1. Make everyone else look lousy.

Apple CEO Steve Jobs' main closer strategy was to offer an insane amount of money compared to other contenders. By making bids that were so irresistible, Jobs perfected the take-it-or-leave-it approach and effectively rendered his subjects blind to any other offer. As a result, he landed basically every deal he wanted.

One such negotiation happened to a music startup called Lala that caught Jobs' eye for its potential to become Apple iTunes. The startup also intrigued Nokia, which offered $11 million, and Google, Jobs' arch nemesis. According to a designer who worked for Lala CEO Bill Nguyen, Jobs wrote down a figure on a piece of paper, passed it to Nguyen and after some nodding, the deal was done. The number? $80 million.

2. Channel your frustration into a well-meaning threat.

After months of public hinting that Microsoft was very, very interested in buying Yahoo!, a frustrated Steve Ballmer wrote a threatening letter to Yahoo!'s board directors, blaming them for a sinking business and offering just three weeks to complete the deal before he would go directly to shareholders—an action he claimed would have an "undesirable impact on the value of your company."

While the letter managed to start discussions between the companies, Yahoo! demanded more than Ballmer could handle and the deal fell flat.

3. Play mind games with everyone.

When Donald Trump decides he wants to take someone's business, he apparently stuffs a few tricks up his sleeve before negotiation time.

First, he'll have his staffers warn you that he's very busy, probably won't be able to stay long and won't shake your hand (he just doesn't do that). Then when Trump enters the room—you know, the one from *The Apprentice*—you're instantly charmed over by his warm handshake, extensive 40-minute chat about business and glossed-over terms of sale.

You walk out feeling quite good about yourself, says a CBS source. In reality, you were duped into thinking completely normal negotiation courtesies were really flattering, undeniably giving Trump the upper hand.

4. Refuse to compromise.

Poor Larry Ellison can't seem to get an NBA team, but that might be because compromise isn't a strong part of his negotiation strategy. While the Oracle CEO has been itching to move a team to San Jose, California, his top picks have spurned him on the basis that they don't actually want to move.

Ellison has been denied the Golden State Warriors, the New Orleans Hornets and, especially, the Grizzlies—on his third attempt, Grizzlies owner Michael Heisley reported, "We're not even considering Ellison. This team cannot be moved." Since Ellison already knew this, maybe he's hoping persistence will pay off.

5. Use prestige as one of your main assets.

Amid the struggling economy and bailouts of 2008, Warren Buffett demonstrated he could negotiate a better deal than the United States Treasury. From a $10 billion investment into Goldman Sachs, Buffett was promised a return that was triple the percentage that the Treasury hoped to get from the nine banks it gave $125 billion taxpayer dollars.

Granted, Buffett was out to make extra cash while the government hoped to save the economy. But really, who would you rather have as an investor? Buffett's name holds prestige none other can match— while his endorsement means impending success, government handouts arguably declare you're on your last leg and no one else would help.

6. Schmoozing pays off.

If you didn't see the Disney-Lucasfilm deal coming, that's because it was kept extremely under the radar. While George Lucas and Disney CEO Bob Iger have been friends and business partners since the 1990s, only recently did Lucas warm up to the idea of selling his beloved company.

Only after Iger challenged Lucas to a mock light saber battle in front of hundreds of cheering Star Wars fans at the opening of a new Disneyland ride did Lucas agree to call him when he was interested in selling. In praise of Lucas's skills, Iger said, "He just has this way of carrying that light saber." After patiently waiting through a year of secret meetings and negotiations, Lucas signed over the Star Wars franchise. Ecstatic, Iger dressed up as Darth Vader for Halloween the next day.

7. Leave lawyers and investors at the door.

When Facebook CEO Mark Zuckerburg acquires a startup, he doesn't seem to like consulting his advisors first. "Mark will convince companies he is going to acquire that they should accept a deal on a projected valuation," one CEO who has negotiated with Zuckerberg told The New York Times. "Then, he'll go back to investors who want to put money into Facebook and say, look, this start-up was going to join us at this valuation, so you should invest at that number."

Then there was last year's $1 billion deal with Instagram, for which Zuckerberg made his lawyers stay inside his home watching *Game of Thrones* while he ate steak and ice cream on the back patio with Instagram CEO Kevin Systrom. Facebook's board of directors was also kept in the dark, only hearing about the transaction a few days before the company's announcement.

8. If cooperation isn't on the table, overthrow the whole thing.

When Dick Costolo became CEO of Twitter, the board of directors was one of many dysfunctional things he inherited. Boardroom leaks were rampant, attendees were openly texting from meetings and there were simply too many people trying to be directors.

Costolo finally got so fed up that he did something not many CEOs have been able to do—he leveraged his authority and kicked all the investors off the board. In doing so, he proved Twitter was *his* company and if you weren't going to play by his rules, he was going to send you home.

9. Remember you have something they want.

Yelp founder and CEO Jeremey Stoppelman held his ground when Google and Yahoo! approached him about buying his online review business. "The negotiation went from looking out and envisioning faster growth, a stronger brand, and more or less local invincibility to a conversation about what the company is worth," he told Fast

Company. "That wasn't why I engaged the process in the first place, so I just shut it down."

Good thing, too, or he may have made an enemy of one of the most powerful men on the planet. While on the phone with an investor and $25 million on the line, Stoppelman was passed a sticky note with the words, "STEVE JOBS IS ON THE LINE." Stoppelman excused himself and switched to his cell phone. "Don't sell," Jobs told him. "Google is evil."

POLARIS
ADVISORY GROUP

Predicting Sales Success in the Hiring Process
<u>What Your Best Salespeople Can Teach You</u>

Our experience in working with sales executives and sales teams have taught us about the importance of knowing what characteristics (innate traits and abilities) and competencies (learned skills and knowledge) salespeople need to be successful. But how do you identify *which* attributes (characteristics and competencies) belong in your sales success profile?

Perhaps the best source, and one that is too frequently overlooked, comes from within your own sales force — your best salespeople. These members of your sales team are very likely to possess the characteristics and competencies that belong in the success profile. The challenge is to identify who those sales team members are, and to isolate and classify the attributes that drive their success. Then you can align your hiring and development programs accordingly.

We recommend a three-step approach — Identify, Isolate, Classify & Align — that can help drive sales success by discovering and leveraging the attributes of your best salespeople.

A few things to keep in mind as you execute each step:

Identify: You'll need to identify a group of outstanding performers, as well as a group of average performers (rather than poor performers) to compare against. When selecting salespeople for these groups, take into account differences in territory opportunity or potential. It's not enough to only rely on performance rankings, competency model assessments, and sales manager input. By assessing territory sales and sales growth relative to market opportunity, you can separate the impact of territory factors from the impact of a salesperson's ability and effort on performance. Most sales leaders think that they know who their best performers are. Yet when they factor market opportunity into the equation, they sometimes discover that the success of a "star" salesperson is in fact driven largely by luck (i.e. a good territory), and not by skill and effort.

©Polaris Advisory Group, LLC

Isolate: Create a list of the attributes that salespeople use to enable their success. You can look at published lists from consultants and research-based recruiting and training organizations, and/or you can ask customers and company sales leaders, managers, and HR experts for input. Observe and gather input about the salespeople in the outstanding and average performance groups in order to evaluate them on the attributes. Then compare the results of your evaluation across the two groups to isolate the attributes that truly discriminate the best from the average performer.

Classify and Align: Your list of discriminating attributes will likely include both characteristics — inherent traits such as high energy level and intellectual capability, and competencies — learned abilities such as selling skills and product knowledge. Classify each success attribute as either a characteristic or a competency, and then align your sales hiring and development programs accordingly. You must hire for characteristics. You can buy (hire) or build (develop) competencies.

The list of success attributes will depend on the sales role. Here is an abbreviated example of characteristics and competencies for a typical sales force:

Characteristics:

- Motivated to succeed
- Ability to work with others as a team

Competencies:

- Ability to understand customer needs and decision processes
- Call planning and preparation with consistent follow-up
- Ability to adapt the company's message for each customer and focus on customer value
- Enlisting the help of other company experts in meeting customer needs

With this information, sales leaders are able to focus sales force hiring around the characteristics, and design development programs around the competencies -- significantly enhancing sales force effectiveness.

We have seen initiatives like these consistently produce bottom-line results. One client we've worked with has been a pioneer in using this approach. Working first with the U.S. sales force, the company identified a group of outstanding performers and isolated a set of "success principles" that differentiated their performance. The company developed a new sales process that was derived from the behaviors of the outstanding performers, and it aligned sales hiring, development, and other programs to support the new process.

A key part of the initiative was using Polaris Advisory Group to develop a selling skills training program called <u>Purposeful Selling</u>. The training produced a more favorable perception of the company's salespeople among customers. The initiative contributed to six consecutive years of double-digit top line growth, well above the industry average. Based on the success in the U.S., the firm replicated the approach globally with similar results.

POLARIS
ADVISORY GROUP

Preparing for the "Solution Economy"

In all varieties of B2B markets have moved beyond selling products and services to offering complete "solutions" to their customers. Alstom keeps trains ready to run each morning for railroad operators rather than just selling the rolling stock to them. General Electric helps hospitals manage and use patient data rather than selling them the equipment and software to do the job. Hilti provides and maintains power tools for builders. Rolls Royce runs the engines you see on the wings of your plane. Syngenta offers rice farmers planted fields.

From the provider's perspective, selling solutions allows companies to differentiate themselves in commoditizing markets and to benefit from economies of scope across multiple profit and service capabilities. For customers, these solutions offer better value than the products and services that went before. After all, who would not prefer a "solution" to their business problems rather than simply buying services and products?

At Polaris, we believe that it is the way of the future and that we are moving toward a "solution economy" where organizations focus on what they are really good at, relying on their suppliers' "solutions" to take care of the rest.

Getting there, however, is going to involve a bigger change than most suppliers realize — most particularly in the way they gather information about their customers.

For a start, there has to be general agreement on what the word "solution" actually means. Customers and suppliers often have different definitions. B2B customers regard a solution as something that helps their business. That is, a solution increases their revenues, lowers their costs, or reduces their risks — and in doing so boosts their overall profitability.

The trouble is, suppliers don't always think about their solutions from that perspective. Many define a solution as a package or bundle of the products and services they already offer. And what they already offer may have no explicit link to an individual customer's business objectives, since the bundles of products and services are constructed to meet generic needs.

Achieving a solution economy will require these providers to change their mindset. But this is not the whole answer. The solution itself has to add real value not seen before. If not, for all the interest shown by the supplier, the customer is going to view the solution simply as a volume discount offer.

Creating that new value will require suppliers to combine their expertise with their understanding of the customer's business needs This calls for changes in how B2B companies gather customer intelligence. Specifically, customer researchers need to:

- **Ask different questions, much more often.** Most companies' customer research focuses on how the customer uses or perceives the supplier's products and services rather than on how these help achieve the customer's business objectives. There needs to be a change, therefore, in the types of questions companies ask their customers and how the resulting data is interpreted.

   What's more, traditional market research is episodic, whereas the nature of solutions requires a more ongoing, relationship-based approach. Periodic market research surveys or focus groups should be replaced by continual data collection, from all interactions between the supplier and its customers.

- **Observe the customer directly.** Solutions often represent major innovations and, as such, customers may not always be able to grasp the value immediately. Traditional research techniques (surveys, focus groups etc.) need to be complemented with observation of how the customer currently operates. And not observation by typical market research or salespeople — rather, observation by personnel with the necessary technical and business expertise to spot opportunities. This is, of course, a challenge when there are large numbers of customers. Technology can help here. One company we know maintains sensors in customers' factories so that it can monitor how the relevant parts of the customers' operations work.

The bottom line is that customer intelligence for the solution economy will look very different from what most companies do today. Customer orientation will become paramount. All customer-facing personnel will be involved; verbal, visual, and quantitative data will flow continually; and this data will be interpreted by people looking through the eyes not just of their company's expertise but also from the perspective of their customers.

Purposeful Selling™

The use of the term "sales professional" is quite intentional. A survey of incoming college freshman were asked what type of job they hoped to get upon graduation. Perhaps not surprisingly, less than 5% of respondents said they wanted to go into sales. Most wanted to become doctors, lawyers, architects, engineers or professionals in other similar professions.

Sales has gotten a bad rap. Maybe this is attributable to such films as "Death of a Salesman" or "Tin Men," an enjoyable and humorous movie about aluminum siding salesmen. Some might even call them "peddlers." Perhaps the image some people have is that of the salesman going door-to-door and selling everything from cleaning supplies to magazine subscriptions.

But sales in today's market – particularly complex sales for high-ticket items with a lengthy sales cycle – involves a great deal of strategy, planning and maneuvering through the many different "constituents" in a large organization. Indeed, we know that these constituents are important in the complex sale – because many people can say "no" and shut down a sales effort, but it's generally a single individual who can say "yes."

Our approach assumes the following:

- That the salesperson is a professional, regardless of the title on his or her business card. Put Sales Representative, Marketing Representative, Account Executive, Account Manager, Business Development Representative – or pick another title. We refer to "sales professionals."
- That sales is an honorable profession and the same amount of continuing education and training that any

other professional would receive should also be available to the sales professional.

- That a seminar, workshop or other one-time event will invigorate the sales professional for a short period of time, but to achieve an enduring increase in sales achievement requires an ongoing process to hone the skills of the sales professional.
- That there is a place for learning "closing techniques" or scripting VoiceMail messages – but that these are ancillary to the broader goal of increasing the level of professionalism which will result in vastly improved sales performance.

The Polaris approach to Sales Professional Development is a process – not an event. And the process is based on the following principles:

1) That customers buy from your company not because of how much they know about your company's products or services, but because of your knowledge of their business and your ability to solve their problems.

2) That selling is "top-down." But before selling to the "top," the sales professional has completed a a great deal of "bottons-up" research into the customer's goals, objectives, strategies, tactics – and the challenges, obstacles and impediments which stand in the way of accomplishing them.

3) When the sales professional does meet with the one person who can say "yes," he or she is so well-versed in the company's business that the decision maker might think the sales professional is an employee of the his or her business!

4) That rather than sharing a laundry list of the sales professional's products or services, only those solutions which help the customer overcome those challenges, obstacles and impediments are presented.

5) That the sales professional is able to demonstrate a solid business case for investing in his or her company's solutions. The customer isn't "buying," but investing – and investments have an ROI, which is part of the business case. And the investment isn't in

products, but in solutions that will solve the customer's problems.

6) Our belief is that the culmination of the research should result in a formal presentation to the decision-maker. And that the presentation should conclude with an assumptive close with next steps and high level action items agreed to. We use the term "assumptive close" because if the sales professional is gaining concurrance to his or her understanding of the customer's business and drawing a correlation between his or her company's solution and the ability for that solution to solve the customer's problems, a "close" shouldn't even be necessary.

Sounds pretty basic, huh? But let's dissect each of these four elements, because when they're presented – more often than not the sales professional's reaction is one of "yawn." In fact, in one meeting with a client during which we were presenting our process, a veteran sales professional was obviously skeptical, and sat with his arms crossed during the entire meeting. His body language silently said "tell me something I don't know." Indeed, even the most junior sales professional knows these truths. But do they "walk the talk?"

In Principle (1), our experience shows that, when meeting with customers, most sales professionals are telling them about their newest product. Or showing them some new, fancy "sales slicks" or marketing collateral. Or telling them about a just-announced price decrease. Rarely are they asking the kind of probing questions which will lead to a greater understanding of the customer's business.

In Principle (2), we know from experience that sales professionals understand that selling is "tops-down." But – in preparation for the "top-down" meeting – rarely does the sales professional conduct the kind of "bottoms-up" research that will identify the customer's goals, objectives, strategies and tactics. And the challenges, obstacles and impediments which are preventing the customer from achieving its goals. This is a skill that has to be <u>developed</u>. In conducting the "bottoms-up" research, most of the people met with don't think in terms of "...what are the goals of your business and what are the impediments to achieving them?" We work with clients to develop these questioning skills. For example, if the sales professional wants to understand the goals of the business, he or she might ask "...I'm curious. If your CEO were to get a report card at the end of the year, what are the things he or she would be graded on?" And to understand the impediments, a question might be "...when your CEO is driving to work in the morning, what do you think are the three things that he's (or she's) concerned about and that are occupying his (or her) thoughts while driving to the office?" Or "...if you had to guess what three things are keeping your CEO awake nights, what would they be?" This type of question-based research (because the sales professional isn't "selling") is very nuanced and has to be developed. Our view is that the sales professional does very little talking and a lot of listening and probing – and will have to resist the temptation to "sell!"

Our observations regarding Principle (3) are that most sales professionals are product-focused. But executives don't care about the features of your company's products. They care about your ability to solve their problems. The sales professional should be able to craft a "solution" – and present a direct correlation from how the solution overcomes the customer's challenges, obstacles and impediments, and thereby leads to accomplishing the business's goals and objectives. If done properly, the natural conclusion is that the customer should invest in your company's solution.

Regarding Principle (4), the sales professional should be able to present a solid business case for the customer to make an investment in his or her solution. From the research completed by the sales professional, he or she should be able to quantify the benefits which result from the customer achieving its goals. These can be increased revenue, decreased cost, reduced Accounts Receivable, a reduction in employee turnover – anything which can be quantified and which supports the customer's goals and objectives. And the sales professional should be in a position to at least estimate the ROI or payback of the customer investing in his or her solution.

For Principle (5), our belief is that the culmination of this research and the associated business case should be conducted in a formal presentation. And that the presentation should conclude with an assumptive close, with next steps and high level action items agreed to. We use the term "assumptive close" because if the sales professional is gaining concurrance to his or her understanding of the customer's business and drawing a correlation between his or her company's solution and the ability for that solution to solve the customer's problems, a "close" shouldn't even be necessary. This presentation should be rehearsed, reviewed with supporters within the customer's organization and that 70-80% of the presentation is reviewing the customer's business and 20-30% is reviewing the sales professional's solution. Again, this is a very nuanced skill which must be developed. Too often, we've seen the sales professional take the approach that, to the customer, sounds like "...let me tell you about your business." Rather, the approach should be to use expressions such as "...based on our research..." and to gain concurrance along the way with questions such as "...is our understanding of your goals and objectives correct?"

Part of our role is to introduce the process. But, unlike workshops, seminars and the like, our consultants actually work with the sales professional in developing a plan to penetrate a customer or prospect. We help in working with the sales professional to complete secondary research about the customer. Moreover, we actually accompany the sales professional on the "research" calls – we don't call them "sales calls." Initially, we may actually lead the call until the sales professional feels comfortable in asking the very nuanced and probing questions necessary to develop a thorough understanding of the customer's business.

After we've completed the secondary research and primary research resulting from our customer meetings, we work with the sales professional in developing and rehearsing the presentation. We even strategize about the best way to get an appointment with the decision maker.

What we've learned through experience is that eventually the sales professional has developed the skills to be independent. But it's not unusual for our consultants to get a call from a sales professional – long after we've completed the sales training and development process – when the sales professional has encountered a roadblock or simply wants to bounce ideas off of our consultants.

We know that our process works. We know that, working with our clients' management team, we can develop the sales professional to the next level: a "Trusted Advisor" for his or her customer. One division president of a multi-billion dollar global petroleum company invited his direct reports to the presentation. After the presentation was completed, he turned to his staff and said, "I wish all of you understood our business as well as this young man does." On another occasion, the sales professional was accompanied by his company's CEO to the Executive Presentation. In front of his CEO, the president of the customer's organization tried to hire the sales professional on the spot (he gracefully declined!). At the conclusion of another presentation, the president turned to a member of her executive team and said "Please assign a project manager to this. And tell whoever you choose that I expect this new production line to be up and running in sixty days." After this, she turned to the sales professional and said, "Nice job. Do you need anything else from me?" The sales professional politely said "No ma'am," after which she said "Please get with my secretary and schedule a weekly meeting so that you can report on the project's progress."

These are not isolated events. But they do demonstrate the power of a process-oriented approach to sales training which provides enduring value for our clients. And as for that veteran sales professional who was so skeptical and sat through our first meeting with his arms crossed the whole time – he became our biggest supporter within his company.

"And old Dave, he'd go up to his room, y'understand, put on his green velvet slippers - I'll never forget - and pick up his phone and call the buyers, and without leaving his room, at the age of eighty-four, he made his living. And when I saw that, I realized that selling was the greatest career a man could want."
Arthur Miller (1915 - 2005), *Death of a Salesman*, 1949.

Quality trumps quantity. Every time.

How much time and money do you devote to your company's sales pipeline? Consider the resources, the software, the meetings, the forecasting, the managing and measuring you do, and the time and effort you dedicate to it. If you're like most CEO's or sales executives, your sales pipeline is your lifeblood. It's what you run your company by; it's how you make decisions, and often it even drives your stock prices. It's your "dashboard."

While the pipeline is a vital tool in managing your business, by placing emphasis on the wrong areas related to the pipeline, not only will valuable resources be misused – both time and money – but you may actually be encouraging behaviors and actions of your sales team which are actually <u>contrary</u> to your real business objectives.

The "conventional" wisdom is something like this: The more calls you make, the more appointments you'll get. The more appointments you get, the more sales you'll close. The more sales that get closed, the greater the company's overall revenues will increase.

While most of the people in your sales organization will not acknowledge this, they (and probably you, too) know that it's true: Most of the opportunities that go into your pipeline are never going to close and should never even have been put in the pipeline. But if we're measuring success by the increase in the number of opportunities in the pipeline, then that's exactly the behavior that will result.

What would happen if the metric we're using to gauge our success is – instead - the improvement of the close ratio for our sales team as a group, as well as for the individual sales professional? Isn't that a legitimate way to achieve the same result: increasing sales?

By using the improvement of this metric as a gauge of success, our focus will shift from maximizing the number of opportunities added to the pipeline to increasing the number of qualified opportunities which get added to the pipeline. If we only add opportunities to our pipeline which are truly "qualified," what will be the result? Less time and wasted effort spent pursuing opportunities which shouldn't even be in the pipeline. An improvement in the ratio of opportunities which close relative to the total number of opportunities in the pipeline. Greater predictability of our top-line revenues as a result of more accurate forecasts. An overall improvement in morale because the time spent "chasing our tails" is either eliminated or greatly reduced.

Intuitively, you know this. In your "gut," you know this. You know this when you make an honest, unvarnished self-assessment of your sales team and conclude that there is built-in dysfunction. "What gets measured gets managed," is the age-old adage. So if we're using the wrong measures to gauge our success, we're naturally motivated to manage the wrong metrics.

The solution? Shift the focus of what you measure to a metric related to the improvement in the quality of the opportunities which make up your pipeline. Your "Win Ratio." The number of opportunities in your pipeline which either "slip" every month or eventually drop off completely from the Pipeline Report. There are a limitless number of possible metrics which are better than simply measuring the increase in the raw number of opportunities which get added to the pipeline.

And if you shift your focus, your sales team will get the message. They'll observe what metrics you pay attention to. They'll notice the shift in the nature of questions you ask in "funnel reviews." They'll take note if the nature of the reports you request from your sales team is different, representing a shift in what's important to you.

Do a little "amateur research" on your own. Take a long, hard look at your top performers and how they spend their time. What do the focus on? Increasing the sheer number of appointments which get set or ensuring that they don't waste their valuable time chasing an opportunity only because it's on the Pipeline Report? Top performers are extraordinarily adept at "separating the wheat from the chaff." Compare their close ratios with those of the overall team. As top-performers, we would expect their ratios to be better than the average. But drill down a little deeper. Are they just naturally more gifted at selling? Do they work harder or put in longer hours? I'll bet you a steak dinner that it's because they don't have a lot of "unproductive" time – time spent chasing opportunities that they know intuitively shouldn't be a part of the pipeline in the first place.

Your sales team needs to be re-oriented. Re-focused. They need to be retrained. They need to know how to identify a "qualified" opportunity against one which is clearly "unqualified." Habits are hard to break. And your sales team, through no fault of theirs, has developed some bad habits.

But your commitment to – and investment in – targeted sales training which will result in breaking bad habits and learning the right habits will demonstrate how serious you are and how important this is. This sales training is not about such esoteric subjects as "reading the decision maker's body language." This is "back-to-basics" training. A focus on the fundamentals. Re-define what makes up a qualified lead. Identify all of the elements and create a qualifying checklist. Ensure that your sales professionals use it!

If you are seriously committed to increasing your firm's revenues by shifting the focus away from raw numbers and on "qualifying" an opportunity to ensure the quality of your pipeline…if you're willing to invest in your sales team by providing them with an affordable and proven training program…if you're committed to assisting in breaking bad habits and learning good habits – or ensuring a change in "learned behavior" through the application of a practical and back-to-basics approach to selling – if you're committed to these, contact us. Our commitment to you is that we won't waste your time or your money. And that we'll be invested in ensuring your success by doing "whatever it takes." Call now. 1-800-320-5368. Or contact me directly via e-mail: gdevitt@polarisadvisorygroup.com.

POLARIS
ADVISORY GROUP

Does Improving Your Sales Force's Effectiveness Require "Evolution" or "Revolution?"

<u>7 Key Levers Available to Management</u>

In the continuous hunt for profitable growth, rarely will "silver bullets" fix problems with your sales force. Most sales force challenges are multi-dimensional. Especially when things are not going well (and sometimes even when they are), sales leaders need to know when evolutionary sales force improvements are enough to drive profitable growth, and when it's necessary to implement a wholesale sales force transformation.

Most evolutionary changes work within the current sales strategy, organizational structure, and sales team. The focus is on getting current sales team members to behave differently. For example, to spend more (or less) time prospecting, to improve customer engagement quality, or to manage the pipeline more effectively. Several operational levers influence sales team activity to help you achieve these ends, including the following:

- **Performance management**: set expectations and manage against them
- **Data and tools**: provide salespeople with insights that enable success with customers

- **Incentives**: motivate high levels of the right sales activity
- **Training and coaching**: help salespeople develop the competencies they need

Evolutionary improvements can also involve minor adjustments to sales strategy (e.g. focus more effort on specific market segments), tweaks to sales force size or structure (e.g. close a vacant territory in a low growth market) or small modifications to hiring profiles (e.g. start screening candidates on technology skills).

But major changes to these more strategic levers require you to graduate your sales force improvement efforts to a more disruptive, transformational change of your sales model and the people on the sales team. Examples include the following:

- **Sales process**: implement a major change to the sales process, such as a move from a relationship-based to a consultative sales process
- **Salesperson profile and recruiting**: recruit a different profile of salesperson and eliminate people on the current team who don't fit the new profile
- **Sales force structure and scale**: specialize (or un-specialize) the sales force or significantly increase or reduce its size, resulting in major realignment of salesperson-customer relationships

Transformational change typically requires a makeover of operational sales force levers as well (e.g. performance management, data and tools, incentives, training and coaching) to keep sales activity aligned within the new sales model.

Sales forces have realized significant performance improvements through evolutionary and transformational change initiatives. Here are two examples.

Evolutionary improvement: Healthcare company Novartis operationalized evolutionary improvement by conducting annual sales force effectiveness reviews. The reviews led to initiatives such as improving customer targeting approaches, and enhancing development programs, coaching tools and performance management processes to reflect the behaviors of top-performing salespeople. These evolutionary improvements contributed to six consecutive years of double-digit top line growth in the U.S., well above the industry average. Many of the improvements were also implemented globally.

Transformational change: Temporary housing provider Oakwood Worldwide implemented a sales force transformation to address changing customer needs that necessitated a move from a relationship-based to a consultative sales approach. It designed a new sales process around the best practices of top-performing salespeople. A large percentage of the sales force did not survive the transformation, but most top performers did. The transformation was supported by changes to operational levers such as sales training programs, coaching processes, and sales enablement tools and metrics. A year after implementation, deal win rates had tripled, sales cycle time had dropped by

50%, and salesperson turnover had declined to under 5%.

Transformational change is usually the best option when customer and company results are seriously threatened, or when an opportunity or environmental factor dictates a drastic rewrite of the sales process. This is easiest to do when you face a crucial event, such as a merger or acquisition, a new company strategy, a major new product launch, a missed financial goal, a change in company leadership, or a major market shift, that acts as a catalyst for change. Transformational change frequently results in a short-term dip in performance, even when done right. You'll get the best results if during the transition you take steps to protect your top customers and your top salespeople who are well-suited to succeed in the new sales model.

Our observation is that the best sales forces make evolutionary improvements *all the time*.

Servant Leadership:
A Path To High Performance

Edward Hess, a Professor at the University of Virginia's Darden School of Business, has spent years researching the DNA of high-performing companies, and surprising, the leaders at most of those companies did not fit commonly espoused theories of leadership.

Many people believe great leaders are charismatic, have a commanding presence, are visionary and educated at elite schools. Almost all of the leaders of the high-performing companies that he studied had none of those traits.

Instead, they are what he calls "servant leaders."

He discovered them while researching well-run organizations such as Chick-fil-A and Home Depot, both based in the Atlanta area, and even the U.S. Marine Corps, headquartered in Arlington. He found them again and again in research done on high-performance organizations such as Best Buy, UPS, Ritz Carlton, Room & Board, Whole Foods, Starbucks, Southwest Airlines, Levy Restaurants, the San Antonio Spurs and TSYS.

Those leaders tended to share common characteristics:

Leading by example

These leaders were servants in the best sense of the word. They were people-centric, valued service to others and believed they had a duty of stewardship. Nearly all were humble and passionate operators who were deeply involved in the details of the business. Most had long tenures in their organizations. They had not forgotten what it was like to be a line employee.

They believed that every employee should be treated with respect and have the opportunity to do meaningful work. They led by example, lived the "Golden Rule," and understood that good intentions are not enough — behaviors count. These leaders serve the organization and its multiple stakeholders. They are servant leaders.

A leadership myth

Many people think that you cannot be people-centric and maintain high standards, because employees will take advantage. That's another leadership myth.

These high-performance organizations show that people-centric environments and high performance are not mutually exclusive. Employees in these companies have high emotional engagement, loyalty and productivity, and outperform the competition on a daily basis over long periods of time. In fact, the relationship between high performance, high employee engagement and how you treat employees is compelling. His research clearly demonstrates that employee satisfaction drives customer satisfaction and loyalty.

Humble wins

Most people seek a leadership position because they want more pay, more prestige, more perks and more power. They seek and fall for the intoxicating powers of leadership.

Servant leaders side step that failing. They are paid more, but very few ever make the highest-paid CEOs list. Instead, they fight elitism in themselves and their organizations. Many of these organizations eschew corporate jets, executive dining rooms, big decorated executive offices and other trappings of elitism. Some of these leaders had small windowless offices. Some shared administrative staff with other executives.

Behaving well

How servant leaders behave is a key to their successful leadership. Behaviors are means of communicating. For example, treating people with dignity, being in the moment and not multitasking, not interrupting others, listening intensely, smiling, saying please and thank you, acknowledging the contributions of others, admitting mistakes, apologizing, not having to be the smartest person in the room all the time and spending time on the front lines with employees and customers.

Servant leaders do not abuse, humiliate or devalue people. They understand that behaviors either build trust or destroy it, and without trust one cannot generally achieve consistent high employee engagement and high performance.

Vigilant leaders

Like behaviors, a servant leader's attitudes and beliefs underpin successful leadership.

Attitudes and beliefs are fundamental because what you think and feel drives behaviors. Servant leaders do not think they are better than the people they lead. Servant leaders do not think that unless employees are watched like hawks, they won't work hard. They believe that if you create the right values and culture normal people will do extraordinary things.

The behavior of leaders, coupled with attitudes and beliefs, either enables or inhibits high performance. Good intentions

and words are not enough. The best leaders understand that daily behaviors count.

The conclusion: leadership is hard work because it takes discipline. Servant leaders are vigilant in fighting elitism, arrogance, complacency and hubris every day – day in and day out.

B2B Marketing: Bringing Clarity To Your Value Proposition

Your marketing strategy is watertight. Your go-to-market plans are honed to precision. Even your budget (for once) is to die for.

And then horror of horrors, your campaign bombs. ROI: Negligible. Embarrassment factor: High. Marketing's reputation: Well and truly tarnished.

The fact is, if your value proposition isn't rock solid compelling, the rest is just plain pointless.

Whether it's a brand, product or service proposition, getting it right matters. But it's also hugely tricky. And we B2B marketers don't seem to do ourselves any favors. As one CIO recently told me (a chap with a multi-million dollar budget under his charge at that): "Most of what I see is just plain confused and confusing."

So where do we all go wrong and what can we do about it? Here are some Earnest rules for creating B2B value propositions that really pack a punch:

Rule 1: Never lose sight of your audience

You may scoff, but many a B2B proposition has rolled off the corporate production lines without any genuine thought for who it's aimed at. And any marketer that tells you 'everyone' shouldn't be in their job. There's nothing worse than propositions that are developed in dark rooms under the misplaced assumption that you know what's best for the customer (okay, one concession it worked in part for Apple).

Before you get to the matter of crafting your value proposition, you need to thoroughly get to grips with your audience. Whether you're into the latest fad for creating buyer personas or not, getting under the skin of the people you want to engage is key. Define who they are, their role in the organization and their drivers. What do you need from a solution? What do you want them to know, think and feel? Can't answer some of these questions? Go and ask them for yourself. A few choice interviews with potential buyers and influencers can prove hugely enlightening.

Rule 2: Never stop looking over your shoulder

Whilst there are some companies that obsess about what the competition is saying and doing – there are others that are strangely ignorant of the messages being thrown by competitors at their target audience. We think it's essential to understand rival propositions vying for customer affections, as its key to building a differentiated message. However, there's a definite case of handle with care. We've seen too many vendors think they need to match the competition word for word – and then add some more. The thinking is, if they're saying that, we've got to say it too. But what can result is uniform blandness. The same buzz words regurgitated albeit in a different order. Here's a simple test: check out the list Adam Sherk compiled on his blog on the most overused buzzwords and marketing speak. Take any one of your value propositions. At a guess, I'll bet you've got a direct match in there somewhere. 'Transform' anyone? Or should that be everyone?

Map out the competition by all means. See what they're championing in their propositions and who they're targeting. Identify where you can carve out a real point of difference. But bear in mind, being better than your competitors at one thing is meaningless if your potential buyers don't place value on it. Finally, don't think once your proposition is created that's it.

Your competitors are likely to soon be fine-tuning their story in response. Today's battle may well be won, but tomorrow is another day.

Rule 3: It's not about what you do; it's about the advantage it delivers

A capability in itself does not a value proposition make. By all means be clear on what your offering is – but articulate the value it brings. Ideally be as tangible as possible. Now we admit, that can be pretty darn hard when it comes to the provision of business or IT services – and when push comes to shove, companies tend to shy away from giving performance guarantees (take Accenture, funny it's "High performance delivered" and not the eminently more compelling "High performance guaranteed"). But if the good folk at IDC would have you believe, tangibility matters now more than ever.

Frugalnomics reigns: "Buyers now seek a quantifiable proof of bottom-line impact, significant ROI, fast payback and superior value from each purchase." Disregard this at your peril. Make a claim and ensure you've got the proof to back it up.

Rule 4: Keep it simple, but not too simple stupid

We're all for simplicity. If you want to surround your proposition in hyperbole and undecipherable technical nonsense, your audience just won't give it the time of day. Think less is more. This is where value proposition development is a real art, knowing which parts of the story actually don't need telling. Take this simple analogy: throw five balls to someone, what's the chance of them catching them all? The same goes with your messages. Too many and they'll fall by the wayside. Better to have one compelling message to lead on that hooks the audience in – and when you've got their attention then you can get down to the nitty gritty.

But a word of caution. Simple is one thing. Dumbing it down is a mighty big mistake. Respect the intelligence of your audience – chances are many are experienced practitioners at what they do. Talk their language and you're more likely to make a lasting impression. Pitch it too low and they'll think your proposition is just too lightweight.

Rule 5: Bring it to life – make it interesting and they're more likely to be interested

We're all human beings - with hopes, dreams, ambitions – however faded and jaded. As much as your proposition is about appealing to the rational business buyer, it's also about making it as compelling as possible to the person underneath – trying to make an emotional connection. Nobody ever got fired for buying IBM and all that. Story telling can play a major part. Translating your dry, one dimensional proposition into a story or scenario that communicates – or better still – amplifies the value you can offer them. Rich media is a great vehicle for doing this. There are examples all over the web. Check out SAP Real Computing. See iRed's simple but effective animations. Or even Common Craft's engaging product explanations. Great for telling the story without boring the pants off your audience – and a fine asset to spread your digital wings all over the web.

Bear in mind these rules and give your value propositions the head start in life they really deserve. As one fine thinker once put it, keep it distinct, make it desirable and ensure its defensible – and you'll go a long way.

The Art of Effective Follow-up

A few months ago, I decided it was time to move forward with a significant home improvement project. I began the process by calling several companies who had done similar work in the neighborhood. Every company was eager to send a representative who spent considerable time with me reviewing the project and gathering the information necessary to submit a proposal.

All of the representatives I met with were friendly and had the expertise and experience I was looking for, and their companies had impressive resumes of similar projects they had successfully completed. I was very clear on how fast I wanted the work performed and everyone agreed that my expectations were within reason. This was going to be a difficult decision…or so I thought.

After all that work, three of the reps were never heard from again. I'm guessing everyone has experienced this frustration, but I'm still amazed when it happens to me.

There aren't many people on earth who have lots of extra time on their hands. Why in the world would a rep invest over an hour with a prospective buyer and then not follow up? Was the project too small? Did something more profitable fall into the pipeline? I guess I'll never know. A quick phone call or email explaining the situation would have gone a long way toward gracefully bowing out and saving your brand's reputation.

While I had some reps bail on me, other reps sent competitive proposals in a timely fashion and then immediately went into hard-close mode. Asking for my business came easily for these reps but asking for my thoughts and reaction wasn't as easy. I started to feel like I was buying aluminum siding and decided that wasn't much fun. So I soon eliminated those reps from further consideration.

What is the "secret" to effective follow-up? And how can you ensure that you don't push too hard, too little or not all at? Here are four simple but valuable ideas to help you improve your effectiveness:

#1.   Don't put it off.

Remember that your prospects are also prospects of your competition. When it comes to follow up, do what you say you're going to do, when you say you will do it, or don't say anything at all! Everyone gets busy and it's easy for follow-ups to fall through the cracks. Don't put it off. Use some form of contact management software to help you track commitments. Don't like what your company uses? Buy your own! It will be the best $200 investment you make this year. The discipline of keeping your commitments costs pennies, but the regret of having them slip can cost thousands!

#2.   Ask great questions!

Most sales people believe that "listening" is the most important sales skill. It's important…but it isn't number one. Asking great questions is the key to moving opportunities forward. "What did you like the best about my proposal?"

What was missing?" "What, if anything, was off target and needs to be re-worked?" "In an ideal world, what would this look like as we move forward?" Follow up is your opportunity to learn and reposition. Don't blow it by forgetting to ask high impact questions. Your goal is not to sell something but to help them make a great buying decision. Remember to keep your focus on them by asking great questions.

#3.   Be persistent, not pesky.

Be sure that you have a good, productive reason for every contact. Not many people are interested in having their sales rep "check in" to see if they've made a buying decision, but they are interested in having you follow up to add value to their decision-making process. Share relevant, new ideas or have one of your existing loyal customers (see all raving fans) call to discuss their experience in working with you. Prepare for every touch point by creating a simple agenda or outline for the conversation. Sharing this with your prospect at the beginning of the call demonstrates that you've done your homework and respect their time. Don't just wing these conversations.

#4.   Just say no!

If, for whatever reason, you decide not to pursue an opportunity, contact the prospect right away and let them know. Introduce them to someone else in your organization or refer them to a competitor. Prospects appreciate the truth just as much as you do. Don't just disappear! Learn the art of a graceful exit and save your reputation and personal brand. Remember that word of mouth marketing is a powerful tool, but it cuts both ways. Everyone appreciates the truth…it's the trademark of a successful rep. Focus on speaking more truth with prospects who aren't the right fit—they will appreciate it and it will free you to focus your energies on other opportunities.

Your ability to master the skill of effective follow-up is crucial to your long-term accomplishments. Most reps are great at the first few contacts, but very few know how to truly nurture an opportunity. Learning the art of effective follow-up builds clients, success and your personal brand.

POLARIS
ADVISORY GROUP

8 Tips to Winning a Sales Fight

<u>(While Maintaining Your Professionalism)</u>

1. You do not talk about "fight club." If you're making the move to fight, don't talk about it internally or externally. If your prospect, your people, or anyone else asks you, the answer is, "We're just working through a few issues right now, but things are going well in general." At some point you will have to play nice with whomever is left standing -- don't gloat to your friends or warn your enemies.

2. Go all Sun-Tzu on them. The ancient Chinese military strategist famously said, "The greatest generals win without battle." Weigh your options one more time. Can you win this deal without a fight? All things considered, it's a better way to accomplish your goals.

3. Never fight "down." If you're going to fight over an issue, go over the person's head. You have one shot at this, and you'll need the most senior person in the room at the prospect's table to exert his or her authority.

4. Just the facts. Your opinions and intentions, the he-said/she-said of conversations -- they all make you look weak. Besides that, your opponent will go back to your supporters at the company after the phone call or meeting and re-tell the story, spinning it in his or her favor.

5. Ask questions, make few statements. Is this how your company normally handles these types of requests? Is this what working together will be like once we close this deal? What parts of your process do we not understand or are failing to fulfill? You want to ask questions, but like a good trial attorney you should know the answers before you ask the question.

6. Concede the little points. There must be some ground to give. Everyone believes there are two sides to the story, so be ready to relent on some issues that are not material but show balance. Stay focused on the issues at the heart of the dispute.

7. Win, don't wound. If you have to fight, play for keeps. You never back a snake into the corner and then turn to walk away. No jabs -- just throw the haymakers, get the issue on the table, and then resolve it cleanly and quickly. Then move on.

8. Leave an exit -- for your adversary. You have to leave a way out for your opponent after you've won the fight. Big companies don't fire your opponents -- they keep them.

.

© Polaris Advisory Group, LLC

POLARIS
ADVISORY GROUP

Stop Managing the Pipeline
<u>Start Managing Your Sales Team</u>

How much time and money do you devote to your company's sales pipeline? Think about the resources, the software, the meetings, the forecasting, the managing and measuring you do, and the time and effort you give it. If you're like most CEO's or VP's or sales managers, your sales pipeline is your life blood. It's what you run your company by; it's how you make decisions, and often times it even drives your stock prices.

While the pipeline is a vital part of the sales process, it is also where the most fundamental mistake is made, and this mistake costs companies millions (if not billions) of dollars every year.

The problem is that most companies spend too much time, money and energy on measuring and managing the pipeline rather than managing and improving the quality of leads that go into - and ultimately come out of - the pipeline.

In other words, most of the leads that go into your pipeline are never going to close, should never have been put in and, as a result, your company wastes hundreds of thousands of dollars generating and then chasing, and measuring and managing leads that will never close. That's the real problem.

Ask yourself: "What is my sales department's closing ratio?" I'll bet you can answer that, can't you? A typical company will report that it takes an average of 50 cold calls or contacts with decision makers to set 15 appointments out of which 10 will turn into proposals or pitches which will result in 1 or 2 sales.

And once this metric is established (as measured by the sales pipeline, of course) the sales strategy is set - to get more sales, you just have to set more appointments. And if you want more appointments, then you have to get your sales team to make more calls! Suddenly everyone works harder, goes out on more appointments, and...and...the desired

results don't come, do they?
And here's why: until you address the fundamental problem- the quality of leads that go into your pipeline - you won't improve your close ratios or your sales. Remember, you can't close an unqualified lead, so stuffing more of them into your pipeline isn't going to get you the results you want. In fact, it will just cost your company more money, frustrate your managers and wear out your sales team.

You've got to stop managing your pipeline and start training your sales teams how to generate more qualified leads. That's the only real answer.

In fact that's the secret of all top sales producers. Look at your own top reps. What are their closing ratios? I'll bet they are the highest in your company, aren't they? They would never consider setting and running 15 appointments because they don't have the time to waste. They would rather spend their time qualifying (I call it disqualifying) out the non-buyers so they can spend their time finding, qualifying and working with real buyers. And they know how to do this because they understand sales. Unfortunately, 80% of your sales team doesn't.

And that's why quality sales training is the only real solution.

But sales training is what most companies don't do well. In fact, if you want to know how well your own sales training is working, simply shop your sales team. Either call in, or get on your lead list and have some of your reps call you. Try throwing them some objections and see how they do. If you're like most sales managers I work with, you'll be appalled by the results.

Again, this is the real problem. Until you solve this basic problem of training your sales team, having them generate and stuff more unqualified leads into your pipeline won't get you the results your company needs. That's why most companies end up spending so much time and effort managing and measuring the pipeline. It's something they know how to do.

If you want to get out of this unproductive cycle and actually start improving your sales and revenues, then here's what you need to do: Get back to the basics of sales training and redefine what makes up a qualified lead. Identify all the elements and create a qualifying checklist. Make your reps fill it out completely before any leads are generated. If you're not sure of a lead, have a manager re-qualify it for them.

The bottom line is you must train your sales force (and sometimes your managers) how to find and qualify real buyers. The more of these you identify and put into your sales pipeline, the more meaningful it will become.

So take the emphasis off managing your pipeline, and start training and managing your sales team. If you do it right, I guarantee you it will finally give you something you'll be happy to measure - more sales!

POLARIS
ADVISORY GROUP

Secrets to Successful Lead Nurturing

Overview

For years, marketers – particularly technology marketers – have been maniacally focused on generating new leads to feed the pipeline needs of their sales counterparts. Unfortunately, only a very small percentage of those new leads, less than 5%, were "ready-to-buy" at the time they were contacted, leading to much frustration and angst between marketing and sales.

So what happened to the 95% of those leads that weren't "sales-ready?" Usually, not much. An occasional e-mail or phone call does not constitute a lead nurturing program that will deliver results.

The benefits of lead nurturing have been well established:

> • Of course, the ROI of lead nurturing depends on a number of things: industry, solution, how much nurturing content is at our disposal, and, of course, the consistency and the quality of our execution of lead nurturing programs.

> • That said, based on an Aberdeen report of complex sales, most companies were able to reasonably expect that 20% of their nurtured leads will convert to sales-ready leads within 12 months.

To accelerate time to revenue, B2B marketers employ nurturing programs that meet the needs of buyers at every stage of the buying process.

What is Lead Nurturing?

So, let's define "lead nurturing:" Lead nurturing is having consistent and meaningful communication with viable prospects regardless of their timing to buy. Simply put, lead nurturing builds solid relationships with prospects, over time, so that your organization is "top of mind" and the clear "trusted advisor" when the prospect is ready to buy.

Benefits of Lead Nurturing

While we intuitively believe that lead nurturing programs will lead to a higher conversion rate from prospects to sales and an acceleration of the sales cycle, we also know the following from a study conducted by Aberdeen Group:

- Only 20% of leads are followed up on;
- 80% of "bad leads" go on to buy within 24 months;
- 80% of sales occur after the 5th contact;
- At any given time, only 3% of prospective buyers are "ready to buy" at the time of contact;
- 40% of leads close eventually, with consistent long term follow-up.

Furthermore, the statistics from those with lead nurturing experience bear this out:

Phil Fernandez, President & CEO, Marketo

> "Companies that excel at lead nurturing generate **50% more sales-ready leads** at **33% lower cost per lead.**"

Brian Carroll, Executive Director – Revenue Optimization, MECLABS

> "Proper lead nurturing programs can yield anywhere from **15% to 200% in additional, new qualified leads.**"

> Our statistics reliably indicate that for every 100 or so prospects nurtured in the prospect pipeline, some 20-40 more sales-ready opportunities will be rendered over time.

Elements of a Successful Lead Nurturing Program

Creating nurturing programs that purposefully impact buying outcomes is achievable with the incorporation of a number of elements:

1. **Put Buyers First**
   As obvious as this is, our experience at Polaris has been that many nurturing programs are designed based on the company's goals, not their buyers' needs. We can tell this because the content and messaging is all about their product offerings. When our prospects are considering change, they've got a lot of questions. Unless they're late in their buying process, those questions are not about the product.

   Our buyers' questions are about clarifying ideas, gaining the knowledge that makes them confident in their choice to move forward and making sure their risk exposure will be minimal. Putting buyers at the center of your nurturing program and designing it to be helpful by sharing valuable ideas that establish the company as the one which "gets" them and is the expert in the field gives them confidence that we can deliver what they need to successfully resolve the issue(s) they're confronting.

2. **Storyline**
   If we know our buyers well, we can design our content touch points to work hand in glove with the steps they take during the buying process. Think about one problem-to-solution scenario and

determine what our buyers need to know to choose to take action. What questions are they asking? Solving problems usually follows a series of (often internalized) questions and answers.

The first question may be, "Why should I change from the solution I already have?" When presented with an answer, usually another question will pop up. And so on as they work their way through solving <u>their</u> issue at hand. We must think progressively and design our content to match.

3. **Create a Dialogue**
   Nurturing programs must be designed to motivate response. If our prospects only engage with the e-mail we send each month, our opportunity to move them forward in their decision to buy from us is limited. A complex purchase is not an impulse buy. Just keeping the your organization's name in front of them is not the purpose of a nurturing program. A nurturing program should be an active contributor in guiding the "problem-to-solution" process.

   The program we develop for your organization should motivate prospects to interact with us. Maybe they read an article and we follow up with an invitation to view a video on the same topic. They watch that and see there's also a webinar that extends the topic and sign up. They attend the webinar and ask a question. Not only do we answer it during the event, but we follow-up with more information afterward to add even more value for them. Each of these interactions is part of the prospect dialogue imperative to building a trusted relationship that develops into a customer.

4. **Pass Along**
   Complex purchases are not chosen by a single buyer. Even if that person is the only one that your sales professional ever meets, there are a number of people behind the scenes influencing the decision. When we plan our nurturing program we

must take into account the people who must be persuaded that your organization's solution is the best choice. Each of them will have a different interest in the project. They'll have differing concerns and expect specific results.

Our content must be designed to answer not just the needs of the *decision makers*, but to be helpful enough to be passed along to influencers. We should design content specifically for influencers and make it available for the decision maker to pass along. We must expand the reach of our nurturing program to as many members engaged in the buying process as possible.

5. **Conversation**
   While there are a plethora of marketing automation firms and solutions – and they have their place – at Polaris we believe that complex sales should involve a human touch at its center.

   Earlier I discussed a "dialogue." A dialogue occurs between people and should be in the form of a conversation. Indeed, the lead nurturing program should be a narrative. That's why we recommend inbound and outbound telesales – often not selling at all, but inviting prospects to visit your booth or a hospitality suite at trade shows, participating in interactive webinars and other activities that incorporate a person-to-person dialogue. This builds trust in your organization, making the prospective buyer ever more confident that your organization should be the vendor of choice.

6. **Consistency**
   Nurturing programs set expectations, make promises and leave impressions. If our content and storyline are fragmented, or if our timing is erratic, our programs will lack the consistency to create the extended levels of engagement. Nurturing programs are only successful when they get buyers to stick with us throughout their buying process.

We seek to build higher levels of participation and engagement over time to get prospects to take next steps with us. Likewise, if the conversations we start diverge from what our prospects expect based on past experiences, we create confusion and doubt about our company's expertise and ability to add the critical value that will deliver a successful outcome.

7. **Acceleration**

   The point of creating nurturing programs is to drive revenue. Staying in touch is nice, but if our nurturing programs are not designed progressively, then our buyers may not take the next steps to move forward in considering us. By focusing our nurturing programs on buyers, the storylines referred to previously that engage them, and the dialogues and conversations that build trust in our expertise, we can help our prospects eliminate the obstacles that stand in the way of their purchase decision.

8. **Transition**

   The buying process is dependent upon transitions. One of the most important ones is the hand off from marketing to sales. Our buyers could care less if they're engaging with marketing or sales, what they care about is the fluidity of the process and the value of the interaction. Marketers who provide their sales teams with the information they need to step seamlessly into the conversation at the hand off will see deals continue to move forward. Those who don't are likely to see stalls when sales comes in blind and starts over like it's the initial introduction.

   Considering that research by Sirius Decisions finds that up to 96% of a company's marketing-qualified leads fail to make it to closure, ensuring that our transition process is seamless is critical.

9. **Technology**

   Since so much of buying is now controlled by our

buyers, and happens online, we've got to have the tools that expand our visibility into our prospects' behavior in response to our content and communications. We've also got to know when they take matters into their own hands and search out more of our content on their own.

Nurturing is a holistic process. It requires continual refinements as we learn more about what's working and what's not and shift our marketing assets accordingly. Following a prospect end-to-end throughout the buying process isn't likely without technology. Learning what salespeople are doing to close deals - or why they're losing - doesn't happen without feedback loops. And prioritizing which prospects are followed up with based on propensity to buy isn't as likely without CRM. Technology can be a valuable enabling technology for nurturing programs that drive sales.

10. **Metrics**
In order to facilitate continuous improvement, we must measure the outcomes of nurturing programs. This requires that we look farther than opens and clicks in emails. Marketers need to look at the interactions they drive with outbound messaging as well as the inbound interactions prospects take of their own volition. We've got to get smarter about what factors actually indicate sales readiness and we've got to learn to measure both long-term and short-term achievements that lead to revenue.

Engagement needs to be thought about as how much time and activity a prospect is willing to devote to your organization over the course of their buying process. By designing nurturing programs across problem-to-solution scenarios, we'll begin to see patterns of activity develop that help us create more momentum in our pipelines. As this happens, we can establish benchmarks and performance improvements that continue to shorten buying cycles - because nurturing programs are finely tuned to meet the needs of buyers every step of the way.

The Impact of Lead Nurturing

For firms which have complex sales, our experience is that most of the selling actually happens when the salesperson isn't with the prospect. And that's where lead nurturing can have a significant impact:

1. Establish Contact Immediately - Establishing contact quickly is key to actually connecting with our leads. An InsideSales.com study found that 35-50% of sales go to the vendor that responds first to an inquiry. And a HubSpot study found that response rates decline as the age of a lead increases.

2. Build Thought Leadership - People do business with businesses they know and trust. While a robust and informative web site can be a critical tool, it's unlikely that prospects will truly understand why they should do business with your firm just from visiting the web site. Lead nurturing is an opportunity to show that we are an expert in our field.

3. Maintain Consistent Communication - 66% of buyers indicate that "consistent and relevant communication provided by both sales and marketing organizations" is a key influence in choosing a solution provider, according to a Genius.com study.

4. Find Segmentation Opportunities – Your organization can learn more about its leads through e-mail nurturing and segmenting our e-mails going forward based on what we learn. MarketingSherpa found that segmented e-mails get 50% more clicks, so any opportunity to segment our leads, we should take.

5. Maintain or Increase Engagement - Lead nurturing is a great way to maintain engagement when a lead has already made the move to interact with us. And, if that lead has stopped visiting your organization's site or reviewing our offerings, lead nurturing is a great way to remind them about our business.

6. Accelerating the Sales Cycle - Market2Lead found that nurtured leads have a 23% shorter sales cycle. Lead nurturing

© Polaris Advisory Group, LLC

is a way for the marketing team to help with the sales process and nurture more leads through the sales funnel.

7. Encourage Referrals and New Lead Generation - Even though we're e-mailing lists of existing leads, lead nurturing has the potential to attract new website visitors and generate new leads. This is the reason that relevant content is critical. If we're doing a good job of sharing valuable content, our leads are likely to forward our e-mail along to co-workers or friends, expanding our reach and attracting new people into your business.

8. Look for Opportunities to Personalize the Nurture - Blend a human touch with our lead nurture projects. For example, place follow-up phone calls after prospects have downloaded a White Paper simply to offer to answer any questions they might have about the subject matter. While the connect rate may be low, a non-sales oriented message leaves a positive impression and increases the likelihood of further conversations and strengthens the relationship with the prospect.

9. Consider Nurturing Existing Clients - Existing clients and customers should obviously be dealt with differently from a lead or a prospect. But as marketers who understand this difference and plan accordingly, we can ensure that our clients are an extension of our sales organization and act as our advocates. Another consideration is the implementation of a nurturing program to up-sell/cross-sell to your existing customer base.

<u>**Lead Nurturing Gone Awry**</u>

As we discussed, there is a fine line between bringing benefits to our prospects and annoying them. For this reason, Polaris recommends that we use a variety of touch points: case studies, press releases, White Papers, webinars, contests, promotions and other means. Our recommendation is that these not be "sales-oriented," but informative and enlightening – that we are demonstrating true "thought leadership." To the degree that the audiences can be segmented by vertical market, we know that this will improve the success of the campaign. Similarly, including well-known subject matter experts and executives from well-known and respected organizations in our program adds to your firm's credibility. This will attract interested parties and avoid the perception by the

prospective buyers that an e-mail from your firm is an "annoyance."

Summary

- Always remember, our lead is not just an e-mail address or a name. They are real people who have their own whims and fancies. Just this small reminder will ensure we are more careful the next time we decide to send the same e-mail to everyone on our list.

- Measure the response of the leads on our list and score them -- and every few months remove those who have been non-responsive.

- If we've been making cold calls or pursuing a lead for a long time, we must ensure that our CRM system reflects these updates and comments so that others on our team have the most current information.

- Make our content easy to read and simple to comprehend. We lose the trust of our leads the moment we send an e-mail with an agenda that's disguised as informative, but is clearly a sales pitch. Let's spell out in clear terms why we've have written to them and what we'd like them to do.

- Spell out clearly how they can unsubscribe to our e-mails.

- Think 'Drip Marketing' – plan how we will slowly nurture our leads and let every communication to them be a value-add building on the prior ones. Receiving the same piece of information again and again can be quite irritating and falls into the category of "Lead Nurturing Gone Awry."

- If we really want our lead to participate in our contests, offers, etc., make it easy for them – expecting people to take too many actions only results in "no response." When planning a promotion, we must remember that our lead is a very busy person. We have to grab his attention and get him to act in the minimum time possible.

B2B Lead nurturing is ideally a marketing process which helps a prospect to make an informed decision. It is a process of educating and preparing a prospect to consider our offerings when he is finally ready to buy because we have gained his trust and demonstrated that we are the "experts" in the field.

The "Elevator Pitch"

Pretend that you are in an elevator at one of your industry's trade shows. You're heading down to the lobby when the doors open on the thirtieth floor. You instantly recognize the executive who walks in and quickly glance at his name badge to confirm he is the CEO of the most important account you would like to start working with. You have never met him before nor have you been able to generate any interest from his organization. You have forty-five seconds to introduce yourself, explain what your company does in a way the CEO would find interesting and applicable, and motivate him to take the action you suggest. Ready? Go!

So, how did you do? Even the most experienced professionals find this pressure-packed exercise difficult. When you're in this situation, avoid the six common mistakes most salespeople make:

They use truisms: They believe their company's own marketing pitch, which makes claims that are not considered entirely true by the listener. As a result, they instantly lose credibility.

They describe themselves using buzzwords: They repeat industry buzzwords or, worse yet, use technical buzzwords that are known only within their company.

They use fillers: They make too much small talk or ask frivolous questions that reduce their stature to the customer.

They demean themselves or the listener: Their statements turn them into mere salespeople, not business problem solvers. They unintentionally demean the listener by asking impertinent questions or assuming the listener knows exactly what they are talking about.

They present an unreasonable close: They don't take into account that they are talking to a senior company leader and use a close that is unrealistic or demands too much of the customer.

They are incongruent: Their tone, pitch, and tempo of speech don't match. They speak too fast and their quivering tone broadcasts that they're scared and nervous.

Here's an example of a poor elevator pitch. The problems are identified in brackets. Luke Skywalker, a salesperson for XYZ Technologies, is attending a trade show and happens to be in the elevator with Norman Bates, chief information officer at Wonderful Telecommunications.

Hello, Norman. How are you today [filler]? Do you have a moment to talk [filler]? My name is Luke Skywalker and I'm a sales rep [demeans salesperson] for XYZ Technologies. Have you heard of XYZ Technologies [demeans listener]? Umm...[filler] Well, we are the leading provider [truism] of business transformational outsourcing [industry buzzword]. We have a unique extended-hybrid implementation methodology [technical buzzword]. Do you have time for me to buy you a cup of coffee and hear more about it [unreasonable close]?

A successful elevator sales pitch will incorporate the following sales linguistic structures:

Softeners: A softener eases listeners into the next thought or is used to set expectations. When you say, "I'm sorry to bother you," you are using the pre-apologizing softener technique.

Facts: A fact is the undisputed truth. Facts are recognized instantaneously.

Metaphors: Metaphors are stories, parables, and analogies that communicate ideas by using examples that people can relate to and identify with. Metaphors enable complex concepts and theories to be explained in an understandable, interesting, and persuasive manner.

Suggestions: Foreground suggestions are direct and explicit ("Consumer Reports gave our product the highest rating"). Background suggestions are indirect and their meaning is inferred ("One of their customers recently switched to our product").

Fallback position: Every customer conversation is actually a verbal negotiation. Instead of giving ultimatums that force the customer to accept or reject your close, provide options from which customers can select from prepared in advance.

Silence: Silence is an important and useful linguistic structure. It indicates you are listening and waiting for a response. Silence can actually be used to gain dominance during conversations.

Here's an elevator pitch that incorporates these sales linguistic structures:

Norman, hi, I'm Luke Skywalker with XYZ Technologies [fact]. It's a pleasure to meet you [softener]. I'm not sure if you are familiar with us [softener], but we work with AT&T [fact]. They've had to reduce their IT costs during these tough times. I'm here because James Bond, the CIO of AT&T, is presenting a case study on how he cut his IT costs by 20 percent using our outsourcing solution [metaphor, background suggestion]. There'll be CIOs from some of our other customers, including General Electric and Johnson & Johnson, speaking as well [fact, background suggestion]. The session is tomorrow at 1:00 p.m. if you can make it [foreground suggestion, softener]. [Pause — silence, waiting for response.] That's too bad [softener]. I'd be delighted to send you his presentation [fallback position, foreground suggestion]. Great. Just to confirm your e-mail address, that's Norman.bates@wonderful.com. Is there anyone else I should send it to [fallback position]? [Pause — silence]. Okay, that's Ferris Bueller, your vice president of infrastructure. Thanks, Norman. You'll be hearing from me shortly.

Your words are your most important competitive weapons. In this regard, your ability to deliver a compelling elevator pitch is crucial to achieve success. There are many sales situations where you have only a minute or two to conduct an entire sales call. You must be able to deliver a compelling and memorable message during this pressure-packed time sensitive encounter.

Write down your elevator pitch and analyze its structure for the use of buzzwords, fillers, and truisms. Use language structures such as softeners, metaphors, and suggestions to improve its persuasiveness. Finally, be sure to practice your pitch aloud so your delivery is smooth and confidant. Remember, a sales call can happen anywhere and at any time. Always have a prepared elevator pitch.

The Universal Laws of Selling

There are many laws of selling that are well known, but people rarely abide by them. Improving the use of even one can significantly improve results.

1. The more people talk, the more they like you.

I'm sure you've heard colleagues lament, "He's nice but he just talks too darn much."

But I doubt you've ever heard the opposite: "Darn, she's nice but just listens too much."

Most people, your prospects included, want to be heard and understood before understanding. Effective salespeople are listening 60 percent to 80 percent of the time, depending on the complexity of their offering. They accomplish this by becoming highly skilled at asking the right questions at the right times. View this need as a fundamental rule of communication.

2. A professional salesperson makes a sales call to be of service to the customer.

If you're making a sales call to meet quota, earn a higher commission, move the "special of the month" or any other reason not arising from your customers' true needs, it's time to check your integrity.

One of the main reasons selling has a negative public perception is too many salespeople sell for their reasons, not their customers' reasons.

3. A qualified prospect has the need, authority and budget to buy.

Ensure the person you're dealing with meets this criterion. If he or she doesn't, find out who does, or you're merely presenting, not selling -- which wastes money and time.

4. No one's born a salesperson.

Similar to every other profession, highly skilled sales professionals have studied and learned their trade. Much as a doctor, attorney or accountant isn't "born," neither is a salesperson.

Abandon this myth and learn your trade. Research reveals that regardless of age, race, gender or experience, a novice salesman with effective sales training can become as successful as his veteran counterpart.

5. What will it do for me?

If the definition of selling could be boiled down to a single sentence or question, this would be it.

Constantly put yourself in your prospects' shoes by asking this question. It will help you focus on their needs and the appropriate corresponding benefits.

6. People don't care how much you know until they know how much you care.

Your prospect must believe that you will do everything possible that's in his or her interest. Without this trust, all the facts, figures and discounts don't mean anything.

Once you gain the prospect's trust, however, you become much more than a supplier -- you become a trusted counselor and partner not easily replaced, despite your competitors' lower price, supposed faster delivery and so on.

7. People buy emotionally and justify logically.

Contrary to what many salespeople believe, this reality actually works in your favor if you've done a thorough job of helping your prospect buy.

It's imperative that you reinforce your prospect's decision to buy with sound reasons for the purchase. If you allow your prospect to buy a new iMac computer because of the cool color -- without reinforcing the time savings, increased productivity and ease of use -- you might as well keep the shelf space open for the return.

8. Send thank-you letters.

Does this really need an explanation?

Send thank-you letters to anyone and everyone -- from the receptionist who set the appointment to each person present for your presentation. Short notes take a little time but show a lot of class. This professional courtesy can open an apparently closed opportunity.

9. Treat every person like the CEO.

It has been said that the true character of a person is revealed in how he or she treats someone who can do absolutely nothing for him or her. Nowhere is this truer than in selling. This makes good sense, because there's the rare possibility the receptionist will someday become CEO.

More likely, you'll encounter many employees who aren't decision-makers but quickly can become part of the decision-making process. You'd be surprised how many deals salespeople have lost by being rude or elitist.

10. Always ask whether anything has changed.

This simple question is imperative and helps minimize surprises. Never assume things are where you left off.
Asking this offers you protection and the opportunity to help the customer know you're working in his or her interest. You might discover the budget's been revised, there's a new time frame or, even that your prospect's company has been sold and all deals are off.

11. Set an objective for every call.

An objective is anything that keeps the sales cycle going -- making a presentation, sending additional information or scheduling a demo. Once the sales cycle halts, it's unlikely you'll get it moving again.

12. Discuss benefits, not features.

This law has become cliché during the past decade, yet most salespeople still don't apply it.

Consider this: There are more than 1 million half-inch drill bits sold annually, but people don't want half-inch drill bits. They want half-inch holes. Show your prospects the benefits of your product or service.

13. Sell value, not price.

Surveys reveal that price concerns often are as low as sixth in the order of importance of prospects. However, it's always one of the first objections raised.

If you're continually locked in price wars, you'll rarely win. You must demonstrate the value of your product or service.

14. Every prospect makes five buying decisions in precise psychological order.

The decisions are about:

- You, the salesperson, including your integrity and judgment.
- Your company.
- Your product or service.
- Your price.
- The time to buy.

Know these buying decisions, and tailor your presentation accordingly.

15. Every prospect buys for one, or more, of six buying motives.

Knowing and appealing to the motives will help motivate your prospect emotionally and logically, moving you closer to a sale. They are:

- Desire for gain.
- Fear of loss.
- Comfort and convenience.
- Security and protection.
- Pride of ownership.
- Emotional satisfaction.

POLARIS
ADVISORY GROUP

Top Twenty VoiceMail Prospecting Mistakes

1. Not leaving one so your prospect doesn't have the chance to return your call.
2. Pretending you have called when you haven't.
3. Not having planned what you want to talk about in advance.
4. Talking about your products, instead of things that matter to your prospect.
5. Speaking for more than 20 or 30 seconds without letting the prospect say anything.
6. Leaving a message that's too short and doesn't give your prospect a compelling reason to call you back.
7. Not showing that you have researched your prospect, and his or her situation, in your voicemail message.
8. Speaking so quickly that you can't be heard. Or worse, mumbling.
9. Leaving a voicemail with lots of verbal pauses (like "ums" and "ahs") that make you sound less confident, and less credible.
10. Leaving a message and then passively waiting for a call back, instead of continuing to try to reach the prospect.
11. Not leaving your name and contact information at the end of the message. Better yet, leave it at the beginning when the prospect is poised to take notes.
12. Sounding too "canned" or "salesy" to catch your prospect's attention.

13. Not mentioning your company's website, if it's your strongest sales tool.
14. Using a tone of voice that suggests you don't expect a call back.
15. Not following up via other means, like email or handwritten note.
16. Giving up too soon, when most prospects won't return your call until you have tried them more than nine times.
17. Not mentioning another company you have helped with a similar problem that the prospect is likely to have.
18. Failing to stick to one topic per voicemail message.
19. Not verifying that you have the right contact before leaving multiple messages.
20. Forgetting to mention a common colleague or someone who has referred you.

POLARIS

ADVISORY GROUP

Value Statements

"What is your value statement?" This critical question is challenging to answer, but doing so strengthens your marketing.

Value statements tell your prospective customer or referral source in a clear and concise way what value you will deliver—how they will be better off after going through your "black box."

Unfortunately, the vast majority of organizations cannot succinctly describe the value their products or services provide. They can describe what they do but not what the essential value is of their services. Most professionals will tell you they know what value they bring, but when asked to articulate its worth, they need three paragraphs to describe it. By then, however, the listener has long lost interest.

Not only does a strong statement help you capture the attention of prospective buyers, but it also goes a long way toward differentiating you from your competition. The advantage will be yours if you can clearly communicate how the customer will be better off because of you, as opposed to simply describing a transaction.

The question isn't whether you bring value, but how to communicate it quickly and clearly. The more succinct something needs to be, the more challenging it is to develop - and the more thought that needs to be given to it. In this way, value statements are similar to taglines - because they're short, they look deceptively simple to create. You see a lot of generic taglines, e.g., "a commitment to excellence," because businesses and professionals give up when they realize the amount of thought, analysis, and cost it takes to develop a worthwhile tagline.

However, value statements often differ from taglines, which have more of a promotional bent. Your tagline may be clever, catchy, and memorable, which is what it should be, but you have to consider whether it conveys what you do and the value the customer will receive from purchasing your products or services. Additionally, your tagline and logo go hand-in-hand in your marketing materials. That's not always the rule with your value statement. There is a place for both taglines and value statements in your marketing program.

Let me interrupt here and say that we can extensively debate the definitions and differences between your value statement, value proposition, tagline, slogans, etc. The definitions vary among marketing professionals. What we're concerned with in this document is how to create your own value statement.

What Do You Do?

To develop a strong statement, begin by answering a few questions, whether individually or in a brainstorming session with colleagues. Consider what you do, and write down the essential value you bring clients. You can have a statement for each service line, then find the common thread and wrap them up into one. Don't censor yourself or your colleagues, and don't stop to wordsmith your thoughts. Just get the ideas flowing. Start with these questions:

- What do we do for our clients?
- Why is that important to them?
- What do they appreciate about our service?
- What is the essential value we're bringing them?
- What does our firm do differently than others?
- Why do our customers think we're different?

In terms of identifying the value you bring customers, you want to dig deeper than just the end result. Consider that the benefit you bring customers is more than what you ostensibly leave them with.

For example, an IT consulting firm gets and keeps a business's systems up and running so that the business owner doesn't have to think about it. The IT firm can also identify efficiencies and help improve how customers use technology. On the surface, that is what that professional is doing. The essential question, though, is: "What ultimate value does this bring the customer?" The real value goes beyond the service provided; it includes the peace of mind that frees customers to focus on other aspects of business. Likewise, the real value of increased efficiency is ultimately a contribution to the firm's revenue potential.

Write down words that relate to the answers to your questions, e.g., efficiency, reduce, increase, smoothly, finely tuned, etc. Think in terms of action words and phrases, such as we generate, we create, develop, reduce, increase, etc.

© Polaris Advisory Group, LLC

Now comes the more challenging part. You want to think about how to distill the answers to your questions into one statement that encapsulates the thoughts you've generated. Your statement should be short and sweet, ideally 10 to 12 words; however, don't worry about the length at this point. Play around with sentences. Again, don't censor. One imperfect sentence can lead to a perfect one. Ask others for their input on what you've developed.

Take a look at your longer phrases and think about how you can further reduce them. Share them with others you trust to get their feedback. Put these thoughts aside and return to them the following day. If you find yourself stuck, you may want to engage professional marketing support.

Here are a couple examples of value statements:

- From author and consultant Andrew Sobel – "I help companies and individuals build customers for life." He uses it as a tagline by shortening it to "Helping Companies and Individuals Build Customers for Life."
- From RAIN Group – "RAIN Group provides sales training & performance improvement for the complex sale."

Begin listening and looking for value statements in other professionals' elevator speeches, websites, etc. You'll see that good ones are hard to find. Once you have your value statement, start incorporating it into your marketing in proposals, on LinkedIn, in other marketing materials, and one-on-one with referral sources and prospective customers.

You can see what a challenge it is to develop a resonant value statement. However, once you do, you have a tool in your marketing arsenal that can cut through clutter and make you heard.

Leads: Are You Making Any of These Ten Mistakes?

Lead Generation Mistake #1: Spending on marketing activities that don't produce an acceptable ROI or are "vanity exercises."

Open up your local business journal, and without a doubt you will see an advertisement for a consulting firm trying to "generate awareness." This organization is "generating awareness" among the 25,000 readers who may (or may not) be targets for its services.

Meanwhile, the funds to create the ad (and to run the ad week after week) can surely be much better spent by reaching out to the smaller, more targeted pool of, say, 1,600 key prospects the firm wants as clients. For the most part, spending on general "awareness" ads produces a very low ROI if any.

Focus your lead generation efforts and dollars on tactics that are going to produce a strong ROI.

Lead Generation Mistake #2: Expecting marketing tactics to produce results without a clear call to action.

Recently, an ad in *Harvard Business Review* for a major consulting firm touting that it was now offering "solutions" versus just "services." Many people saw that ad. And almost all did nothing because they were asked to do nothing.

If, however, the ad had focused on new research in intellectual property protection for technology companies that could be downloaded as a white paper, the ad could have been used to generate leads for the firm.

People will accept an offer-white paper, case study, article, book, research or even a sales call from an ad. They will rarely, if ever, pick up the phone and go from reading an ad to becoming a new client.

Have a goal, a clear call to action and an offer for each of your marketing tactics.

Lead Generation Mistake #3: Not implementing any lead generation tactics because of inefficient decision making.

We've met with many firms to talk about lead generation, and these companies are "hot to trot" with their lead generation efforts - they want more leads and they want them now! Then, six months go by, a year goes by, three years go by, and they still have done nothing.

All too often, there are too many decision makers who can't get on the same page and decide what to do when it comes to marketing and lead generation. So, they end up doing nothing -- or even worse, running another awareness ad in the business journal.

If you find yourself complaining about a lack of leads, yet unwilling to move forward with any lead generation campaigns, either stop complaining or do something about it.

Lead Generation Mistake #4: Not being able to sustain implementation over the long-term.

As much as you might like to shorten the sales cycle, buying complex, trust-based services takes time. Leads need to be nurtured over the long term so you are top of mind when the elusive time of need arises.

All companies want more leads and want them now. As a result, they plan and implement a lead generation campaign, but they impatiently "dig up the roots of the tree" after two weeks to see if it's growing yet.

Lead generation efforts must be sustained over months to make them 1) work, and 2) improve over time.

Lead Generation Mistake #5: Relying on one tactic only.

In *Managing the Professional Services Firm*, David Maister lists "first string" marketing tactics, which include small scale seminars, speeches at client industry meetings, and proprietary research. Maister calls direct mail and cold calls "clutching at straws" tactics. By themselves, they are. Very few prospects will go from receiving direct mail, an e-mail, a cold call, or even a first conversation to immediately becoming a client.

But the best way to get people to take advantage of those "first string" offers is a combination of "grasping at straws" tactics.

Lead Generation Mistake #6: Poor implementation.

Suppose you decide to run a small-scale seminar (a "first string" marketing tactic). You spend months preparing the content, practicing your delivery, putting together the invitations, and booking the facility. Then, the day comes and only a small handful of people show up. So, what happens? Invariably, you give up on seminars and declare, "We tried that, it didn't work."

On the contrary, seminars can and do work, you just implemented the marketing of the seminar poorly.

A number of tactics can be successful to generate new leads for your products or services. Know what it takes to successfully implement each tactic. And if you don't know what it takes, get help from someone who does.

Lead Generation Mistake #7: Dropping leads and failing to nurture leads.

According to a research report by BPM Forum, over 80% of generated leads are never followed up on, are dropped, or are mishandled.

It's also the prevailing wisdom that with proactively generated leads, 25% are short-term, while 75% are long-term. If you're focused on the short-term, you might be missing out on three-fourths of your opportunities.

Don't let leads fall through the cracks! Develop a long-term nurturing plan to win your fair share of the 75% of prospects who are not ready to buy right now.

Lead Generation Mistake #8: Not communicating the value in marketing.

Marketing departments want to be perceived by their constituents (internal and external) as credible and distinct, so they end up writing marketing messages that say, "I'm credible and distinct." Or, "I'm trustworthy." Or, "I'm innovative, yet solid."

If you want your clients and prospects to believe you are credible and distinct, you must <u>demonstrate</u> that you are credible and distinct. You can do this by providing value directly in your marketing and selling efforts. When you interact with your constituents, or communicate any message to them, they're evaluating what it might be like to work with you. Help your internal and external constituents understand that working with you <u>after</u> they've engaged your services is much the same as what it's like working with you before they became your constituent.

Lead Generation Mistake #9: Not integrating various marketing tactics well.

Lead generation is a multi-step process. It takes multiple touches to draw prospects into the seduction of your services. These touches need to be well-planned -- with a consistent message, at the right frequency, and with the right mix of offers. Not all prospects will be interested in attending a seminar or reading a White Paper. Others will want to do both before engaging in a conversation with you.

Consider this: do you think a prospect will accept a meeting with you from a cold e-mail? Probably not. But will that same prospect provide you with their contact information in exchange for a new White Paper that is relevant to their business? Probably. And will they accept a follow-up call to discuss the content of the White Paper -- or an in-person meeting to discuss how the topic applies to their business and situation? More often than not, the answer is yes.

Integrate your lead generation efforts – and include multi-channel, multi-touch and *consistency* for the greatest success.

Lead Generation Mistake #10: Planning poorly for lead generation.

Value-based marketing. Consistent messaging. Integration. Targeting. Lead nurturing. All of that is for naught if it is not well-planned, measured, and tested.

Planning for lead generation and *what to do with the leads generated* is not a one-time event! When it comes to marketing and lead generation, some tactics work better for some companies than others - and you never know which ones work best for you until you test them. Thus, we recommend that you "mix it up" in the modes of communicating with prospects.

POLARIS
ADVISORY GROUP

Wanna Ensure I Won't Buy What You're Selling?

Like most of you, I get cold calls and e-mails every day -- not spam, I mean "real" sales calls -- most of them for things in which I have no interest, or for which I am not even a prospect. And like most people, I almost never answer or respond. It's not because I have it in for all salespeople -- though probably most of us have a hard spot in our hearts for solicitations -- it's because the vast majority of them botch their door-opening efforts so badly.

I appreciate that these people are doing their jobs and trying to make a living. In fact, as I remind myself, whenever I get a call, e-mail or message from a salesperson, I remind myself that at my company, and probably yours, we call people to try to sell stuff, too. So I'm not insensitive to the plight of the honest, hardworking sales professional.

The problem is, most of their hard work often goes into turning me off to the point of nearly total disinterest in whatever it is they're selling, even if they were straight-up giving away gold bullion. As I delete the emails and voice mails, I invariably wonder, "Does this stuff work on anyone?" I suppose it does, or they wouldn't keep doing it, but it's hard to imagine many of these players have a high batting average.

I'm referring mainly to business-to-business pitches, including:

Acting too casual or familiar: I can't tell you how many salespeople open with some iteration of "Hey, George, how've you been?" First of all, saying "how've you been" when we've never even spoken before is disingenuous and sneaky; it's a subtle tactic designed to make someone just unsure enough to not hang up. But once I figure that out, the chances of the call going anywhere are hovering around zero or less. To use formal business terminology, I find it yucky. *Click.*

Leaving "mystery messages:" This one almost cracks me up, if it weren't so sad. It's where a salesperson leaves a message with no message: "Hi, this is Joanne, please return my call at your earliest convenience at 800-555-5555." I get at least one of these every couple of months. Seriously, does any real, credible sales prospect actually return a message like that? I suppose a vulnerable individual or a rookie might do so, perhaps worrying about the unknown, but an ostensibly savvy business person? *Delete.*

Being misleading about the genesis of the contact: "Someone mentioned your name to me" -- really, who? "I believe you expressed some interest in our product a while back" -- no, I didn't. "I studied your website and noticed you're not being found in web search results" -- if you actually studied our site you'd notice otherwise. And my favorite, "I'm not calling to sell anything" -- um, yes, you definitely are. *Dial tone.*

Don't "BS" smart, busy people. If your job is to cold call, do it with class and honesty. Try, "I'm hoping you'll allow me to introduce myself," or even better, actually know something about your prospect and say something targeted and specific: "I see you make laptop bags" – which in this fictional example happens to be true -- "and am hoping you're open to looking at a new material we've developed" -- we are, send me your info!

Being presumptuous with follow-up expectations: This seems to be an increasingly popular tactic -- sending an email or leaving a phone message with a specific appointment time: "Please confirm that you're available for a brief introductory call on Wednesday at 3:00 p.m." You don't know me, we've yet to even speak, I haven't expressed interest in what you're selling, and you're penciling something in my calendar?

It sounds harmless enough, suggests initiative, thoroughness and tenacity. But it also crosses the chutzpah line. *No sale.*

Scorn really isn't my default emotion when it comes to salespeople; sales make the world go 'round and we all want great sellers working for us. But these pitches sound and read like they came out of some horrible "get rich selling stuff" seminar.

I fully understand the classic rules of selling: build rapport, get 'em interested, overcome objections, get to "yes," ask for the order and so on. But taking these rules too literally is self-defeating. Put that age-old wisdom in your tool box, but lead with sincerity, respect, honesty, and a likable and real personality. You're still going to get doors shut, phones hung up and e-mails deleted, but probably not quite as much. Just as in customer service, authenticity and empathy shine, even through phone lines and ethernet cables.

Clearly the deck is stacked against cold-call selling, even at its finest. Like mailing a million catalogs to get a 2 or 3 percent response rate, it's one of those businesses where you accept a lot of rejection in the hopes of getting enough fish on the hook to make it worthwhile. But by breaking free of a mechanical, insincere approach to selling, getting off-script and thinking like one human reaching out to another human, you can improve those odds. In a low percentage game, even one more successful call makes a big difference.

7 Reasons (Some) Customers Dislike Salespeople

A recent research project identified eighty (yes, 80!) reasons that customers either dislike salespeople or responded that they definitely wouldn't buy from them based on various factors. Here's the "Short List:"

1. Not listening. This was the most cited reason customers dislike salespeople. Too many salespeople neglect to listen to what their customers or prospects say, which means they fail to address the key issues that their customer has stated as being important. I remember an interaction with a couple of salespeople a few years ago. One of them asked some great questions to learn more about my particular situation. However, his counterpart did not listen to my responses, and as a result, his solution did not address my business challenges and buying requirements. In fact, his presentation was so far off base, I abruptly called an end to the meeting. Time is a precious commodity for people and when you don't listen you disrespect your prospect.

2. Talking too much. It still amazes me how many salespeople think that "telling is selling." I see this in virtually every type of sales environment from B2B to B2C to Retail. Our view is that your prospect or customer should do most of the talking in a sales conversation. Salespeople react to this idea by saying, "But if they're doing all the talking how can I sell my product?" The key is to let your customer do enough talking so that you can properly present a solution to their problem or situation.

3. Lack of knowledge. In today's information- rich world, there is no reason for a salesperson to lack knowledge about the products and services they sell. I know that the life-cycles of many products are very short and that many companies introduce new products at an alarming rate. However, if you don't know enough about your products, you are going to lose your customer's respect, and in all

likelihood, the sale. Do yourself a favor and invest the necessary time learning about your products and services.

4. Lack of follow-up. Many salespeople say they will do something and fail to follow through. This ranges from promising to get information to taking care of a problem or concern. Many people use this as a barometer before they make a final buying decision. Here's an example:

> A potential customer asks for a particular piece of information and the salesperson promises to deliver it by a certain date. The deadline passes and the prospect has to call and remind the salesperson. Because the sale has not been finalized, warning signals go off in the customer's mind. After all, if the salesperson is this slow to respond BEFORE the sale is made (the courting stage), how long will it take him to respond AFTER the sale?

Lack of follow up results in lost sales. A person contacts two or three companies about a particular item or project. All three submit a quote but only one makes the effort to follow up. Which is more likely going to get the sale?

5. Lying. "I don't care about the customer and I'll tell them anything I have to in order to get the sale." Believe it or not, I heard this comment from a participant in one of our sales training workshops. Unfortunately, the number of sales people who lie or intentionally mislead their customers is

staggering. This behavior includes: overstating the capabilities of your product, stretching the truth, or giving people the wrong information. Almost everyone has bought a product from someone who was less than truthful, and as a result, has become more skeptical with their buying decisions.

6. Failing to understand the buyer's needs. This is an extension of the first two reasons customers dislike salespeople. When a sales rep talks too much and listens too little, they don't get a full understanding of their prospect's situation. I have worked and interacted with hundred – if not thousands – of salespeople over the years, both as a trainer and a buyer. I can state without hesitation, that a mere twenty percent of them actually take the time to

understand their customer's needs, situation, concerns, etc. And it's this group of individuals who are the most successful.

7. Refusal to take 'no' for an answer. Almost everyone in sales knows the importance of persistence. However, there is a fine line between being persistent and being a pest. While you shouldn't drop your efforts after the first 'no,' it is critical to recognize that you won't gain anything by pressuring people. In many cases, the reason someone says 'no' is because they don't see the value in your product/service or because they are not a highly qualified prospect.

Why a "Sales Call Strategy" is Key

It's the question that goes through the mind of a salesperson during every call: How is the target reacting to my pitch?

It's an apt question. In my win-loss analysis interviews with more than a thousand key decision makers about <u>what determines success or failure in sales</u>, I routinely ask at what point in the sales cycle the salesperson actually lost the deal. The most frequently mentioned response is during a sales call. With this important turning point in mind, let's examine how to develop a winning sales call strategy.

Customers will have one of five different reactions to everything you say during a sales call. They will either reject your statements and ideas outright, ignore what you say, acknowledge they've heard you, accept what you say but do nothing, or internalize your recommendations and take action. The reaction you receive is influenced by the level of rapport you have established with the prospective customer.

Similarly, sales calls can be classified by the level of rapport.

Combative sales calls are antagonistic interactions with nonexistent rapport. Most likely, this type of situation occurs because the customer has a preexisting bias against your solution or an incompatibility exists between you or your company and the customer.

Contentious sales calls may begin congenially but are characterized by controversy or topical disputes that lead to ill feelings by the end of the call.

Unemotional sales calls lack outward displays of affection, and even though the call may last an hour, the customer remains aloof and unsympathetically distant.

Friendly sales calls are situations where the customer is generally receptive, cooperative, and open to your ideas. However, this doesn't mean they will buy your solution.

In *synergistic* sales calls, the customer shows genuine excitement, is receptive to your advice and recommendations, and jointly plans the future steps of the sales process with you.

Customers can experience many different types of reactions to salespeople, ranging from fear and hate to love and trust. For example, combative and synergistic sales calls are at the extreme ends of the spectrum. The winning sales call strategy is based upon executing synergistic sales calls and this is dependent upon establishing four different receptive states with the prospective customer.

Personal receptive state. The first priority is to build a personal receptive state by finding intersecting activities and interests you have in common with the prospective customer. By doing so, you develop rapport with the entire person, not just the business person--building a personal friendship that sets you apart from the competition. Collect personal information about the evaluators through research, casual conversations, and quick examinations of the pictures, objects, and mementos in their offices. Always, preplan how you will create a personal receptive state at the beginning of the sales call.

In addition, speak in the customer's unique language. Match the tone, tempo, and speaking style of your customer to make him or her feel more comfortable. The most important difference between you and your competitors is not solely your products, your company, or the services and support you offer. It's you and your ability to build a deeper relationship with prospective customers.

Technical receptive state. Every industry has developed its own language to facilitate the mutual understanding of terminology and an exact meaning of the words. The "technical specification language" consists of these abbreviations, acronyms, and specialized terms. Whether you are selling airplanes, computer chips, or telephone equipment, you need to know the terms and nomenclature of your industry.

A critical aspect of the sales call is not necessarily what you have planned to say on your call or in your presentation. Rather, it is how you handle the tough questions the customer asks you. Your question-handling ability is what helps separate you from the pack and this requires you to speak fluently with the customer in the technical specification language.

Business receptive state. When you demonstrate that your primary interest is in the customer's success, you begin to build a business receptive state. At this point, the customer starts to consider you more than a vendor. You have proven your value as a business partner who has the expertise to solve the customer's problem.

One of the main traits of top salespeople is language specialization because a "specialist" beats a "generalist" every time. Instead of the recitation of standard "generic" product features and functions to the customer, the business receptive state is based upon a tailored discussion about business process improvement that is specifically applicable to the customer's environment.

Political receptive state. You enjoy a political advantage over the competition when the customer believes that only your solution will help him achieve his personal benefactions. The term "benefaction" refers to the psychological benefits that determine a person's actions. It literally means receiving a benefit from taking action. Four core psychological drives determine selection behavior. People buy products they believe will help them fulfill deep-seated psychological needs: satisfying the ego, being accepted as part of a group or becoming the leader of it, ensuring survival, and avoiding pain. Customers rationalize their political decisions with logic and facts from the technical and business receptive states.

As a sales call progresses, continuously ask yourself if you are establishing the personal, technical, business, and political receptive states. A synergistic sales call occurs when all four receptive states are achieved whereas friendly sales calls may only have personal and technical receptive states established.

Finally, be sure to prepare your colleagues who will join you on the sales call by helping them understand what type of sales call to expect (combative, contentious, unemotional, friendly, or synergistic) and their role in executing your call strategy. Never forget, one of a salesperson's deadliest sins is to chatter and talk incessantly on sales calls. You have conducted the perfect sales call when you have listened far more than you spoke.

©Polaris Advisory Group, LLC